No One Can Travel Through God

INSPIRATIONAL CHRISTIAN PROSE POETRY BY

RICKY CLEMONS

PUBLISHED BY FIDELI PUBLISHING, INC.

ISBN: 978-1-970730-83-8

Published by

Fideli Publishing, Inc.
119 W. Morgan St.
Martinsville, IN 46151

www.FideliPublishing.com

Table of Contents

No One Can Travel Through God...1

Does Anyone Own Their Life? 8

God, Himself, was Born in a Manger 10

The Light...14

Who Can Be More? 21

The Beyond Existed Before 26

In the Wintertime of the Heart.................................30

Limit...32

We Can Only See the Visible Things.................................35

So Pure 38

The Hardest One to See 40

Only God Has the Right to be God.................................42

The Lord Can 44

Not Always Peaches and Cream 46

Even When Things are Not Going Well 48

This Life is Nothing Good Compared To.................................49

Regardless Of 50

Rejection Can Be a Blessing from the Lord 53

Physically Sick and Spiritually Sick.................................55

Love 57

Will Go On...62

We are No Match for the Devil.................................64

Spiritual Things are the Best Blessings 66

No One Can Escape from Time 67

Life Will Not Always Be Easy 69

Up in Heaven 71

Everybody is Important to Jesus...73

The Days Were Created on Earth 75

The Good Guys to Win...78

What Good Is...80

Jesus is Our Only Guarantee..82

There is Nothing Wrong with Jesus...85

True Love is in Actions 87

The Spiritual Career is Eternal 88

For Granted 90

Doesn't Come Anywhere Close..92

So Naked Before the Lord 93

As You and I Draw Closer and Closer to Jesus............................95

Divorce Can Come From 97

The Christian Man and the Man of the World 100

If You and I Harden Our Hearts... 102

Without Your Approval, My Lord 106

Like We've Never Been Through 108

We Church Folks 110

If You Put Your Trust In... 114

A Stranger... 115

I Live in a World 117

Heavyweight 119

With Their Words 120

There are People Who Will 121

Trauma Can Shatter 123

When Jesus Comes Back Again 125

God Will Take You and Me to His Court 129

Don't be Deceived 131

It's Easy to Believe 133

Everybody Can Choose to Believe in Jesus Christ 135

Those Kinds of People 137

We Can Only Take 139

All the Good and Right that I Do 140

We Can't Do Anything About 142

Has Been Around for Thousands of Years 143

The Greatest Gift in the Church 144

I Miss Them So Very Much, O Lord 147

There's Nothing Wrong About 149

An Abundance of Life 151

I Want to Walk in Your Holy Spirit, O Lord 153

Sometimes When I 154

The Side Effect of Life 156

There are People Who 158

Jesus Can 159

We Can Want to Rush 160

Being Real 161

I Will Know and They Will Know 163

The Righteous and the Wicked Alike 165

We Can't Get Ahead of God 167

Don't Believe that You Can 169

Sin is Sin in the Presence of God 171

The Devil Has Deceived So Many People 172

Only Here on Earth 174

O Lord, You Created Everybody Different 176

Overlook 178

The Mind is Very Powerful 179

It Doesn't Take Much Effort 181

There is Only One Salvation 182

Will Worship 184

There is So Much Stuff 186

The Only Way 187

I Feel Like I was Right There 189

A Big Heart 192

Spiritually Charged Up 194

There are People Who Believe 195

There are People, Even in the Church 197

It's So Easy 199

Doing Something Good for the Wrong Reason 203

What was the First Sin on Earth? 205

Behind the Curtains of Life 208

It's Always Good 210

The Church is for Sinners Like Me and You 211

Spiritually Oppressed 213

Because of You, my Lord 215

Nothing Can 216

No One Can Travel Through God

Who can travel through God and come out of God to end up in another place?

Many people in this world will travel from city to city and will get tired.

Many people will travel from state to state and will get tired.

Many people will travel from country to country and will get tired and need some rest.

No one has yet traveled through the outer space that looks so eternal and has no end with stars and galaxies.

So, who can travel through God who is bigger than billions of universes and trillions of galaxies that can't travel through God and come out of God to end up in another place?

Lucifer could not travel through God to come out of God and end up self-existing above God.

No one can travel through God and come out of God to end up in another place outside of God.

No atheist has yet traveled through God and come out of God to end up in another place so it could be true for them to say there is no God.

God allows atheists to believe that there is no God, but they only delude themselves and end up at a dead end that doesn't exist in God.

Who can travel through God to come out of God and end up in another place outside of God?

If no human being can travel through the outer space, then how can we travel through God and come out of God to end up in another place outside of God?

The heavens cannot contain God because the heavens can't travel through God and the heavens would not even dare to try it.

All the angels in heaven know that Lucifer failed to be like the most-high God who created him and all the angels who didn't exist before God who had self-existed way beyond trillions of years ago before He created the angels.

No one can travel through God and come out of God to end up in another place outside of God and live to tell about it.

That's something no angel can ever do.

Billions of universes and trillions of galaxies and all things that exist that God created would get very tired and worn out and cease to exist anymore if they tried to travel through God.

They would truly fail in the presence of God, the only self-existing One because nothing was ever before God.

The unfallen worlds won't dare to question God about His self-existence that no one can ever travel through and come out of God to end up in another place outside of God.

The devil and his angels can't travel through God to come out of God and end up in another place outside of God.

This means they cannot escape from hell that God created to cast the fallen angels into as well as all who are lost in their unrepentant sins.

No one can travel through an all-present and non-ending God who is very present in countless universes and galaxies and unfallen worlds beyond this sinful world.

No one can travel through God and come out of God to end up in another place outside of God who is all-present over wickedness to destroy it in fire and brimstone that can't travel through God and come out of God to end up in another place outside of God.

Therefore, the wicked can never escape from God's great judgment and wrath.

No one can ever travel through God's holy word and come out of God to end up in another place outside of God's holy word that is about good and evil in this world.

God will judge good and evil in His holy place up in heaven and not in another place that doesn't exist outside of God.

No one can travel through an all-present and all-powerful never-ending self-existing God who sent His only begotten Son, Jesus Christ, to this sinful world to save us from our sins and redeem us back to God.

Only Jesus can travel through God, and only Jesus is worthy to travel through God because Jesus is One with God and self-exists with God.

No other celestial, terrestrial or human being can be One with God.

No one can travel through God and come out of God to end up in another place outside of God that Jesus Himself couldn't do to not drink the cup of God's wrath to save us from our sins.

The sins of the world couldn't travel through God and come out of God to end up in another place outside of God to give the devil the victory over us to be lost in our sins.

Jesus' mission was predestined up in heaven for Him to shed His blood on the cross and die on the cross and be raised from the grave to let the devil know that he can never go to a place outside of God to escape from his eternal punishment by God.

No wolf in sheep's clothing in the church can travel through God and come out of God to end up in another place outside of God and have the Holy Spirit of God.

No one in this world can travel through God and come out of God to end up in another place outside of God's love.

There is no other place outside of God's love to give us world peace when sudden destruction comes upon this whole world one day according to bible prophecy that was given to us out of God's love to warn us to repent and turn to His Son, Jesus Christ, before it's too late.

All the light years in billions of universes can't travel through God and surely the speed of light can't travel through God who is eternally all-present and surrounds all existence.

No one can travel through God except God's Son, Jesus Christ, and the Holy Spirit who are One with God in the trinity Godhead.

Even the angels can't ever fathom the self-existing One and are not worthy to travel through God.

No angel, no creature in unfallen worlds and no human being can travel through God and live to tell about it.

No one can travel through God and get to a destination where God is not there to evaporate anyone into thin air that can't travel through God to become visible to you and me.

No one can travel through God and prove that God doesn't exist and live to tell it.

No one can travel through God and end up in another place outside of God who is everywhere at the same time so no one can get by Him with their false theories and false doctrines.

No one can travel through God.

Lucifer believed that he could travel through God and get to his destination outside of God to exalt himself above God.

Lucifer failed to do this because it was impossible for him to accomplish that.

The impossible can't travel through God to reach its destination of possibilities outside of God.

No one can travel through God and get to another place outside of God and exist in the presence of a self-existing God who even eternal death can't travel through and come out on the other side of God because there is no other side that exists outside of God.

Nothing exists beyond God.

No one can travel through God and be sane to tell about it because Lucifer became insane because he believed that he could take God's place on His holy throne.

Lucifer could not rise up outside of God as he had traveled from the highest heaven down to the unfallen worlds where God was all-present.

Lucifer and his lies couldn't travel through God and get to anyplace outside of God to deceive all existence with his lies about God.

No one inside the church and outside the church can travel through God and go to a place outside of God's salvation to enter into heaven without believing in his Son, Jesus Christ.

If you and I can't travel through time that is so full of anything that can happen to you and me at any time of the day and night, then we surely can't travel through God that time can't travel through and come out on the other side of God for anyone to have unlimited time to be saved.

So, who in heaven and in the unfallen worlds and here on earth can travel through God and come to a place outside of God and still exist in God's presence?

Only Jesus Christ and the Holy Spirit can accomplish that because they are also God, who no angel and no creature can travel through and go to another place that doesn't exist outside of God.

God is eternally everywhere at the same time, but hell for the wicked will only be in one place that will be eliminated by God on Judgment Day that can't travel through God and come outside of God in another place for the wicked to live forever in their sins.

No one can ever travel through God who no fallen star can fall through and end up in a place outside of God, who circles forever around the countless universes and galaxies and unfallen worlds and black holes that are like a pebble in the sand that God holds in His eternal, unmeasurable hand.

No one can ever travel through God the Father, Son and Holy Spirit who created all existence and can create new existing things beyond countless universes and galaxies and unfallen worlds and black holes that can't end up in a place outside of God.

No other place exists outside of God, who can travel through time to give us borrowed time to be saved in His Son, Jesus Christ, before it's too late.

No one can travel through God and live through it, and no man can travel through the universe and live through it.

God surrounds the universe that can never exist in a place outside of God, who is the self-existing One, to not exist in a place outside of Himself that doesn't exist.

Atheists have the nerve to try to make their big bang theory exist outside of God, who their false theories can't travel through and go to a place outside of God to eliminate God from the church.

No one's thoughts, words, imagination, pride, feelings or actions can travel through God and end up in a place outside of God's presence.

No one's technology, science, medicine, artificial intelligence, invention, magic, luck, wish, education, opinion, theory, physique, psychology, interests in politics or plans can travel through God and come outside of God to end up in another place to be more genius and more powerful than God.

No one's good looks, dreams, visions, fantasy, greed, prejudice, skills, hatred, envy, jealousy, anger, strife, wealth, wars, crimes, lawlessness, immorality, favoritism, victories or injustice can travel through God to come outside of God to end up in another place when God is all around this sinful world day after day for nothing to get around Him and exist longer than an eye blink that is much less than one second that can't travel through God and end up in another place outside of God.

No one can travel through God and end up in a place outside of God.

There are film makers who will portray an everlasting place, a paradise to travel to in the outer space that will run out of existence before it could reach to the end of God where nothing else exists except God.

Eternity can't travel through God because eternity is like only one inch long compared to an immeasurable God who created eternity with one spoken word outlasting all existence below God's everlasting holy throne.

No one's brilliance and great mind can travel through God and end up in a place outside of God who doesn't overlook the simple who God can use to confound the genius who can't travel through God and end up in a place outside of God to have more knowledge, creativity and wisdom than God.

Psalm 90:2-7v, Psalm 93:2v, Psalm 102:11-12v, Psalm 146:10v, Psalm 148:1-13v, Revelation 22:13v

Does Anyone Own Their Life?

Does anyone own their life and get to live it any kind of way and think that God will overlook it like He is not affected by how anyone lives their lives?

Does anyone own their life and think they can take their own life like God didn't give them breath to breathe to live?

Does anyone own their life and think they can leave God out as if God doesn't care to be in their life?

Does anyone own their life and think they can live it like there is no God to answer to, especially on God's judgement day?

Does anyone own their life and think they can treat it like God has no say-so about their life?

Does anyone own their life and think they are right to live it unto themselves and that God is wrong to interfere?

Does anyone own their life and think they can shorten it like God doesn't see it and show any mercy on anyone to live another day?

Does anyone own their life and think they can stop God from overriding their comings and goings here and there that God can take to the dead-end grave?

Does anyone own their life and think they can live it wild and dangerous like God has no laws to abide by for the good and well-being of their life?

Does anyone own their life and think that God's salvation doesn't exist at all for anyone who chooses to live for His Son, Jesus Christ, before it's too late to be saved?

There is no eternal life in living your own life that is like a shadow passing over the landscape that will disappear, but God is eternally all-present and owns all the living and all the dead to judge so fair according to how everyone who ever lived their life from the beginning of this world to the end of this world.

Does anyone own their life and think they can save themselves from death as if there is no God to disapprove of anyone's life being cut short for His reasons that are always right?

Does anyone own their life and think they can give up on their life as if God can't come into anyone's life right on time to change anyone's life so they live it doing His holy will that is right for anyone to live by with no regrets or belief that God is wrong to own anyone's life?

Does anyone own their life and think they can take someone's innocent life and believe that God is all right with it?

God will not allow anyone to get away with murder, no matter how rich anyone may be.

Does anyone own their life when God gave His only begotten Son, Jesus Christ, to die on the cross to save us from a life of living in our sins that can cause anyone's life to be lost for not believing in Jesus Christ who is the creator of all life?

No one owns their life because God owns all lives to shorten or prolong and no one in this world can override or stop God from following through on making His final decision upon anyone's life to be blessed by Him or cursed by Him.

Does anyone own their life and think they can live it beyond the existence of destiny as if God didn't create a destiny for anyone to choose in their lives?

Does anyone own their life and think they can live it like there is no goodness of God that can lead anyone's life to repent and turn to His Son, Jesus Christ, to live a renewed life that God owns beyond the old sinful life that sin owned to cause anyone's life to be lost and lose out on everlasting life that God owns through His Son, Jesus Christ?

Does anyone own their life and think they can curse God and die like Job's wife said to Job whose wife didn't own her life to be angry with God who owns all thoughts, words and actions that God knows to come from anyone before anyone knows what they will think, say and do?

God, Himself, was Born in a Manger

God, Himself, was born in a manger.

How can it be possible that a God in heaven was born in flesh and blood?

When God, Himself, was born in a manger, all that was predestined by God flashed by eternity like a car's lights flashing by a window in the night.

When God, Himself, was born in a manger, time stood still and could not move ahead of God to follow through on His mission to save sinners from being lost in our sins.

When God, Himself, was born in a manger, the mother of God greatly cheered all the angels and unfallen worlds because she was chosen by God to give birth to Him in the flesh that is forever below His self-existence in the Godhead of His Son and Holy Spirit who are three persons in one God.

It is an eternal deep mystery that God, Himself, was made flesh that only God could have lived forever in because God had no sins in His flesh at birth.

Because of the first Adam's disobedience against God, all human beings are born in sin to die, even up until today, but God, Himself, became the second Adam and was born with no sins in His flesh because God was born of the Holy Spirit and a virgin mother who knew no man before God was born.

It was like God, Himself, had stepped down from His holy throne and left all of heaven to become a human being like you and me so He could relate to us and we could relate to Him whose purpose is to save us from our sins, which the devil hates.

It was like God, Himself, died on the cross and then God raised himself from the grave, which only the true living God could do because God is the self-existing One in the trinity Godhead.

No angel and no creature in the unfallen worlds and no human being in this sinful world can fully understand that God, Himself, is the totality of possibilities and nothing is impossible for God.

God, Himself, was born in a manger because God and His Son and the Holy Spirit is God who said, "Let us make man and woman in our likeness."

Only God, Himself, can be three persons in one trinity Godhead.

Our minds are too limited to fully know the self-existing God, just the same as the angels and unfallen worlds can't know Him.

God has everlasting love for all that He created He came down very low to be born in a manger that was forever far from God's eternal palace in heaven, just so that He could live among fallen sinners like you and me who deserve to die and be lost in our sins.

God's love for us existed before His grace that originated from God's love for all the world that God, Himself, overcame in the Garden of Gethsemane where God drank the cup of His wrath so you and I could escape His eternal punishment in fire and brimstone if we believe in God's Son, Jesus Christ, who is God Himself.

God, Himself, was born in a manger because no one can separate God the Father, Son and Holy Spirit from each other.

They are the self-existing one who was wrapped in swaddling clothes in a manger that defines this poor, sinful world that needs a savior God to save us from our sins.

Three persons in one God have different functions but they all were together to move upon a virgin young woman and have her give birth to a God who came from heaven at the fullness of time to fulfill all the prophecies in the bible.

Jesus is God who was born in a manger that became a paradise to all who were there to welcome baby Jesus to this sinful world where God, Himself, was with Jesus and in Jesus to be the self-existing God laying down in a manger.

Even the animals knew He was the only living God who created them to be there at that special, eternal moment in time.

God, Himself, was born in a manger because God the Father, Son and Holy Spirit were never separated from each other in the womb of a virgin mother who an angel from heaven spoke to about her giving birth to the Son of God who was God Himself in Mary's womb.

No one can fully understand the three persons who are one self-existing God who came down from heaven to fill a virgin's womb with salvation for all men to be saved in a God who had said before Abraham, "I am."

That was Jesus saying those deep words to the Jews because Jesus was God, Himself, who was born in a manger to be like the deepest mystery that no one can solve but God Himself.

The three persons in one God cannot be separated like it was from the beginning that God said, "Let us create male and female in our image," which comes to show that Jesus was God and was in on the creation of Adam and Eve.

Jesus was also God who was born in a manger from his self-existing creation of a miraculous birth of a God child from the womb of a virgin mother that only God, Himself, could do to be God in the flesh as His Son, Jesus Christ, who is God, Himself, in the Alpha and Omega and I am that I am who was before Abraham.

The three persons in one Godhead may surely be like each body part having a different function on one body, and that is the same with God the Father, Son and Holy Spirit being three persons in one God, Himself, born in a manger where there was no separation in the trinity Godhead filling up the virgin Mary's womb with God, Himself, who is the creator of the heavens and earth that the God Jesus created for Himself who was God, Himself, born in a manger.

God, Himself, is God the Father, Son and Holy Spirit who is three persons in one trinity Godhead, and one can't do anything without the others because there is no eternal separation between them.

They all had an active part upon the womb of a young virgin woman to give a miraculous birth to a God to be born in a manger where God, Himself, was still in the trinity Godhead to fulfill His mission in the flesh to be like us and save us from our sins that the God Jesus never committed against Himself who is God, Himself, who was born in a manger.

Genesis 1:26, 27v; Matthew 1:18v-4:13-17v-28:19v; Luke 2:6, 7v; John 1:1-18v-8:56-59v-10:29-33v; Colossians 1:15-20v; Hebrews 1:1-14v-2:1-18v; I John 5:7, 8v; Revelation 22:1-13v

The Light

The light can show you and me everything that we need to see, whether it's the big things or the small things, we can see them in the daylight.

The light is always good for our eyesight every day, and we can do a lot more thing in the daylight than we can in the dark night.

The sunlight can surely energize us to move here and there and almost everywhere, especially in the light.

The sunlight can cause us to feel so much better in the early morning light after the dark night passes over us.

The light can shine so bright, even in a light bulb that can brighten up a dark house so you and I can walk into it and maybe see little crawling bugs trying to hide from the light.

When we turn on the lights in our house, the dark disappears as if it was never there in our house.

Many people can work much better in the daylight than in the dark night.

Many people can drive much better on the roads in the daylight than in the dark night.

Many people can do a lot of things much better in the daylight than in the dark night.

Soldiers can surely fight in a war much better in the daylight than in the dark night.

The sunlight is much more beneficial to anyone than the dark night, just like it was proven to the Hebrew soldiers back in the bible days.

The Lord made the sun stand still in the middle of the sky and delayed it going down to extend the day so Joshua and his soldiers could win the war against five Amorite kings that were hiding out in a dark cave because they had lost the war against the Hebrew soldiers who the Lord God was on their side under the sunlight.

The devil hates the light of the world who is Jesus Christ who came down from heaven and was born of the Holy Ghost and a virgin mother in a dark, sinful world.

You and I can see everything all around us in the light, and we can surely see even ourselves in the light, but we can't see everything all around us in the dark night.

We can't even see a little bug that is crawling on the ground when it's dark.

Jesus foreknew that the devil's dark sins would blind many eyes in this sinful world so they would not see the light of God's truth that Adam and Eve rejected in the Garden of Eden where God spoke to them and told them not to even go anywhere near that tree of knowledge of good and evil.

The light of God had shined so bright all through Adam and Eve before they chose to disobey God who is eternal light beyond all the shining stars in the outer space.

One day soon, there will be a light that will shine so eternally bright to cause all the wicked living to drop dead and all the righteous living to be changed from mortal to immortality and all the graves will be opened for the righteous dead to be raised up in that bright eternal light shining on the clouds of glory.

Jesus is that eternal bright light that the bible tells us about.

Jesus is there for you and me to live in the light, and we can choose to do that in this dark, sinful world that will get darker in sin before Jesus comes back again.

Jesus gives His light to shine in you and me to win souls to Him who is the light of the world to see the gospel of Jesus Christ shining so bright in His salvation that He gives to all the world.

No one can live in too much of the devil's dark sins for Jesus to not save us from our sins if we repent and turn to Him.

Even if we are not aware of a dark sin that we are living in, Jesus can bring it to the light for you and me to see that dark sin so we can confess it and repent and turn away from it.

The light will not cause anyone to stumble or fall down, but the darkness will sooner or later cause anyone to stumble and fall down.

The devil and his angels know this all too well because they are doomed to be thrown into the darkness of hell for rejecting the light that they could never overshadow and put out of heaven or on earth.

The light will help you and me to see who is living in the darkness of complaining.

The light will help you and me to see who is living in the darkness of gossiping.

The light will help you and me to see who is living in the darkness of telling lies.

The light will help you and me to see who is living in the darkness of adultery.

The light will help you and me to see who is living in the darkness of pride.

The light will help you and me to see who is living in the darkness of fornication.

The light will help you and me to see who is living in the darkness of holding grudges.

The light will help you and me to see who is living in the darkness of envy.

The light will help you and me to see who is living in the darkness of covetousness.

The light will help you and me to see who is living in the darkness of selfishness.

The light will help you and me to see who is living in the darkness of delusion.

The light will help you and me to see who is living in the darkness of deception.

The light is always a good thing to shine in the dark to help you and me to see where we are at and where we are going.

Without the light of God's holy word, we can't see the spiritual pathway that leads us to Jesus who overcame the darkness of sin for you and me to live in the light of His victory over death and the grave that is filled with the totality of darkness upon the wicked dead for being lost in their sins.

You and I can see everyone and everything all around us in the light of the day, until the dark night comes in and we have to turn on our lights in our houses so we can still see.

If we have a power outage, that lets us know how important it is to have light, even in our houses, for us to see so that we don't stumble over something and fall down and hurt ourselves.

The light can surely motivate us to want to move around and go here and there because we can see without a doubt where we want to go and where we may need to go, especially to the household of faith.

The light can surely show us ourselves in the mirror all day long, especially in the mirror of God's holy law that is spiritual light that will help us to see our dark sins.

In a dark house, we can't see ourselves in the mirror until we turn on the light in the house.

Only God turned on the light in this dark world of sin when he gave His only begotten Son, Jesus Christ, to light up this dark world with God's love for all the world to be saved in the light of only one salvation that is Jesus Christ who we can all believe in to be saved from our dark sins.

A light will surely shine in the dark for us to see what is in front of us and behind us as well as beside us and beneath us wherever we go.

A light will surely shine in the dark that will disappear even in the mere light of a candle that can give us enough light to go from room to room in a dark house.

That candle light can light everything up for us to see what is in every room in the house.

Only Jesus Christ is the light of the world, because Jesus shines God's light of love all around the world.

Jesus Christ is the head of the church and makes His church shine the good news about Him to all the unbelievers so they can come out of the darkness of living in sin and live in His light that the darkness can never cause to black out in Jesus' true children who shine their lights in this dark world through their love for one another to be Jesus' disciples in this dark, sinful world.

Whatever anyone thinks, says or does in the darkness of sin will come to the light of God's judgment, beginning with anyone in the church who will be judged first.

God will judge all the world and it will know the light of His truth and will know that God is fair and will make the right call about anyone's destiny, to be heaven or hell.

In the dark night the moonlight and the stars can shine their light up in the sky.

In the daylight there is no way for the dark to appear up in the sky and black out the bright sunlight, which goes to show that the dark can't block out the light in the day.

Fire can give us light and warmth on a cold night, and fire can burn its light in a fireplace to keep us warm.

Electricity can give us light with a light bulb so we can see in our houses at night.

The batteries in our vehicles give us light on the road so we can see where we are driving in the dark night.

The light is a lot more useful to us than the dark all around the world.

Jesus Christ is the light of the world to save all souls from being lost in the darkness of sin that is very useful to the devil and his fallen angels, as well as to anyone who loves to live in the darkness of sin.

The dark cannot eliminate the light of God's love that shines in a blind man's heart, and he will shine his love and obedience unto God in a dark, sinful world where a blind man will see the light of God's truth for believing in Jesus Christ.

The spiritually blind will stumble and fall down into the darkness of sin, while the righteous blind man, woman, boy and girl is walking day by day in the light of being saved in Jesus Christ.

Only the light of Jesus Christ will shine so bright and cause the living wicked to drop dead while the righteous living will look into the light of Jesus Christ and be changed from mortal to immortality.

There was a time when Jesus became the darkness of sin on the cross, and Jesus said to His heavenly Father God, "Why has thou forsaken me."

But that darkness fled from Jesus like a scared mouse when Jesus rose from the grave to light up the lives of all who believe in Him to be saved.

The light will always be the right way for you and me to truly see one another from day to day.

The light of God's holy word will also help us to see the truth about those of us living in the darkness of sin or living in the light of Jesus Christ who has no darkness in Him.

Jesus is the light of the world, shining over every soul so all can be saved before it's too late to choose to live in the light of Jesus Christ.

We can see our moles, scars, sores and freckles on our skin in the light but not in the dark.

The dark doesn't make these things disappear from our skin just because we can't see them, because the darkness cannot get rid of what we see in the light.

The light shows us real proof of what is all around us from day to day until the dark night comes in and we can't see what is all around us.

In the dark we can't even see a spider that crawls so near to us because we can't see in the dark.

The same thing applies to you and me who can't see anyone for who they are if we are living in the darkness of sin, but living in the light of the truth of God's holy word will help us to truly see anyone either being like Jesus or being like the devil.

The devil can appear to be an angel of light and you and I wouldn't recognize him if we are living in darkness.

Only God's children of light can see right through the devil and know that he is evil all the time with no light of any good thing in him.

Who Can Be More?

Who can be more wise than God and live another second?

Who can be more loving than God and live another second?

Who can be more trustworthy than God and live another second?

Who can be more wealthy than God and live another second?

Who can be more truthful than God and live another second?

Who can be more giving than God and live another second?

Who can be more vibrant than God and live another second?

Who can be more knowledgeable than God and live another second?

Who can be more beautiful than God and live another second?

Who can be more peaceful than God and live another second?

Who can be more fast than God and live another second?

Who can be more strong than God and live another second?

Who can be more balanced than God and live another second?

Who can be more respectful than God and live another second?

Who can be more just than God and live another second?

Who can be more skillful than God and live another second?

Who can be more gifted than God and live another second?

Who can be more joyful than God and live another second?

Who can be more powerful than God and live another second?

Who can be more heartbroken than God and live another second?

Who can be more talented than God and live another second?

Who can be more humble than God and live another second?

Who can be more great than God and live another second?

Who can be more kind than God and live another second?

Who can be more gentle than God and live another second?

Who can be more free than God and live another second?

Who can be more friendly than God and live another second?

Who can smile more than God and live another second?

Who can listen more than God and live another second?

Who can talk more than God and live another second?

Who can reason more than God and live another second?

Who can be more successful than God and live another second?

Who can be more plain than God and live another second?

Who can be more encouraging than God and live another second?

Who can be more motivating than God and live another second?

Who can be more protective than God and live another second?

Who can be more brave than God and live another second?

Who can be more supportive than God and live another second?

Who can be more patient than God and live another second?

Who can be more perfect than God and live another second?

Who can be more on time than God and live another second?

Who can be more genius than God and live another second?

Who can be more right than God and live another second?

Who can be more wonderful than God and live another second?

Who can be more glorious than God and live another second?

Who can be more magnificent than God and live another second?

Who can be more superb than God and live another second?

Who can be more superior than God and live another second?

Who can be more supreme than God and live another second?

Who can be more alive than God and live another second?

Who can be more high than God and live another second?

Who can be more poetic than God and live another second?

Who can be more seeing than God and live another second?

Who can be more complete than God and live another second?

Who can be more jealous than God and live another second beyond God's jealousy over all of those who love Him and keep His Commandments?

Another second can't even be more time for a fool to live and repent and turn to God if it's too late.

No one can be more holy and righteous than God who gives more time to a fool to repent and live another second in His presence, who the speed of light can't keep up with and will never be faster than God and still exist.

Our Witness of Jesus

The devil loves to destroy our witness of Jesus before unbelievers day after day.

You and I who are Christians are supposed to be a witness of Jesus Christ to anyone we come in contact with.

One day in the morning I went to my local post office to get my refund from my mail that didn't get to its destination on time.

The post office clerk said to me that he didn't have any cash to give to me, so he printed out a money order and handed it to me.

He told me to write my name on the money order where it said "pay to" and put my address where it said "from" on the money order.

He also told me to come back to the post office the next day and he would have the cash money to give to me in return for the money order.

I went back to the post office the next day and another post office clerk said that she didn't have enough cash to give me what I was owed.

She told me to come back later that day and she might have enough cash to give to me in return for the money order.

The devil was trying to tempt me to get angry and say something wrong so that he could destroy my witness of Jesus before the post office clerk who had served me many times in the past.

The Lord showed me that the devil was behind it all and was trying to discourage me and make me act in a way that was not like Jesus before the post office clerks.

If I didn't stay in prayer without ceasing, the devil would have succeeded in causing me to say something that would destroy my witness of Jesus.

Thanks to my Lord Jesus Christ, the devil failed in this, because the Lord strengthened me so I could be patient with the post office clerks until they could give me the money that was due to me.

My witness of Jesus was not destroyed because I listened to and obeyed the voice of the Holy Spirit telling me to stay calm and say nothing so I would not cause the post office clerks to believe that I was a hypocrite.

Our witness of Jesus will be tested anywhere and any time when we least expect it.

If we don't stay in prayer day after day, the devil will tempt us to give into his temptations to ruin our witness of Jesus, and this can even happen right in the church.

The Beyond Existed Before

The beyond existed before any vision.

The beyond existed before any creativity.

The beyond existed before imagination.

The beyond existed before any word from the tip of a tongue.

The beyond existed before any action.

The beyond existed before any theory.

The beyond existed before educated guess.

The beyond existed before any wish.

The beyond existed before any dream.

The beyond existed before any opinion.

The beyond existed before any luck or magic.

The beyond existed before any atheist.

The beyond existed before any mental, emotional, psychological, physical and spiritual raging storm.

The beyond existed before any genius.

The beyond existed before any substance.

The beyond existed before any matter.

The beyond existed before any element.

The beyond existed before any oxygen.

The beyond existed before any breath.

The beyond existed before any movement.

The beyond existed before any education.

The beyond existed before any psychology.

The beyond existed before any physics.

The beyond existed before any philosophy.

The beyond existed before any big bang theory.

The beyond existed before any seen thing.

The beyond existed before any unseen thing.

The beyond existed before any design.

The beyond existed before any activity.

The beyond existed before any law.

The beyond existed before any book.

The beyond existed before any second, minute, hour, day, week, month and year.

The beyond existed before any time.

The beyond existed before any life.

The beyond existed before any wealth.

The beyond existed before any light.

The beyond existed before any darkness.

The beyond existed before any power.

The beyond existed before any evil.

The beyond existed before any kingdom.

The beyond existed before any nation.

The beyond existed before any people.

The beyond existed before any animal.

The beyond existed before any reptile.

The beyond existed before any creature.

The beyond existed before any insect.

The beyond existed before any technology.

The beyond existed before any science.

The beyond existed before any medicine.

The beyond existed before any doctrine.

The beyond existed before any light years.

The beyond existed before any black hole.

The beyond existed before any war.

The beyond existed before any choice.

The beyond existed before any free will.

The beyond existed before any achievement.

The beyond existed before any reward.

The beyond existed before any idea.

The beyond existed before any hero.

The beyond existed before any warrior.

The beyond existed before any beauty.

The beyond existed before any error.

The beyond existed before any flaw.

The beyond existed before any mistake.

The beyond existed before any winner.

The beyond existed before any king.

The beyond existed before any president.

The beyond existed before any doctor.

The beyond existed before any surgeon.

The beyond existed before any pilot.

The beyond existed before any engineer.

The beyond existed before any judge.

The beyond existed before any lawyer.

The beyond existed before any author.

The beyond existed before any publisher.

The beyond existed before any athlete.

The beyond existed before any actor.

The beyond existed before any business.

The beyond existed before any builder.

The beyond existed before any military.

The beyond existed before any marriage.

The beyond existed before any family.

The beyond existed before any holy saint.

The beyond existed before any angel.

The beyond existed before any unfallen worlds.

The beyond is God who is self-existing beyond anything in the outer space.

The beyond is God who is the beginning and the end beyond trillions of galaxies and billions of universes that God can create over and over again beyond this fallen world where sinners are redeemed back to God through His Son, Jesus Christ, who is also God as well as the Holy Spirit who is the beyond.

The beyond is God who is love in His self-existence before He created all things for His purpose.

In the Wintertime of the Heart

It can get very cold in the wintertime, and sometimes it will get below zero degrees in some towns, cities and states.

It can get so very cold that it causes power outages in some places and many people have no heat in their houses to keep them warm.

It can get so very cold in the wintertime and cause some people to get frostbite and even trench foot that is never a good thing for anyone.

It can get so very cold in the wintertime and cause tree limbs to break off the trees and ice to coat power lines and make them fall down on the ground.

In the wintertime of the heart, many people will blame God for the loss of their loved ones.

In the wintertime of the heart, many people will turn their backs on the Lord if they are going through some hardships in their lives.

No winter season can get colder than a very cold heart that can cause many people to kill other people.

No winter season can get colder than a very cold heart that can cause many people to scam so many other people.

No winter season can get colder than a very cold heart that can go below the degrees of hatred, envy, gossip, greed, murders, cheating, lies, deceptions, covetousness, robbery, arson, complaining and sexual immorality.

No matter how cold the heart gets, Jesus can warm it up like the heart was never frozen in sin if there is true confession and repentance in the heart that turns to Jesus, who is our spiritual sunlight who shines his warmth of love all through our hearts.

There is nothing Jesus can't do for anyone, even in the wintertime of their heart.

Jesus can heat up the coldest heart with love that He showed to all the world on the cross that He hung on and died on and rose from the grave with the victory over death to give us eternal life over the cold wintertime of the heart.

We all have experienced a wintertime of the heart in some kind of way, but Jesus' gives us His warmth of salvation for all to be saved in Him who cannot fail anyone, to give us a warm heart of love for everyone.

If we are saved in Jesus, He will warm up our hearts with His mercy and grace because He does not want us to be lost in our very cold sins.

Limit

Everybody has a limit to not go over from day to day.

Everybody who drives on the road has a limit to not disobey the laws on the road.

Many people have driven on the road and gone over their limit and gotten killed in an accident on the road.

Everybody doesn't know their limits, so God winks His eye at them and spares their lives from death.

A limit can surely let you and me know not to walk down a dark road at night.

A limit can surely let you and me know not to put our hands in a burning fire.

A limit can surely let you and me know not to jump into a deep swimming pool if we can't swim.

A limit can surely let you and me know not to co-sign for someone, especially if we don't know them.

A limit can surely let you and me know not to get in the middle of a couple's arguments.

A limit can surely let you and me know not to walk towards a poisonous snake, especially if we see it.

A limit can surely let you and me know not to do anything too fast that can cause us to injure ourselves.

A limit can surely let you and me know not to go anywhere near a bear's cub.

A limit can surely let you and me know not to make an angry man or woman more angry.

A limit can surely let you and me know not to try to run across the street through busy traffic.

A limit can surely let you and me know not to get up out of our sick bed and go to work.

A limit can surely let you and me know not to get into debt.

A limit can surely let you and me know not to laugh with a fool.

A limit can surely let you and me know not to eat too much food.

A limit can surely let you and me know not to get drunk and drive.

A limit can surely let you and me know not to represent one's own case before a judge without a lawyer.

A limit can surely let you and me know not to tell someone how to run their business.

A limit can surely let you and me know not to keep company with an enemy.

A limit can surely let you and me know not to make the same mistakes.

A limit can surely let you and me know not to try to make friends with an angry man or woman.

A limit can surely let you and me know not to keep lending money to someone who won't pay it back.

A limit can surely let you and me know not to be who you and I are not.

A limit can surely let you and me know not to go somewhere that we know is full of trouble.

A limit can surely let you and me know not to leave our vehicle doors unlocked at any time of the day and night.

A limit can surely let you and me know not to tell our business to an enemy.

Everybody has a limit they know not to cross over, no matter how bold they are.

Everybody has a limit they know not to cross over, no matter how genius they are.

Everybody has a limit they know not to cross over, no matter how rich they are.

Everybody has a limit they know not to cross over, no matter how wise they are.

Everybody has a limit they know not to cross over, no matter how good they are.

Everybody has a limit they know not to cross over, no matter how foolish they are.

Even God has a limit up in heaven that He cast Lucifer and his angels out of, because God wasn't going to allow Lucifer to pollute heaven with his sins forever and ever.

Jesus had His limit to not let the merchant exchangers pollute His house of prayer, so he cast them out because they were cheating the poor out of their money.

A limit can surely let you and me know not to make a vow with God and then not keep it because sooner or later we will deeply regret it.

We Can Only See the Visible Things

We can look all around us and only see the visible things day after day, and we see visible people and animals.

We can look all around us and only see the visible things day after day, like we see visible insects and reptiles that we don't usually like to see coming from anywhere close to us.

We can look all around us and only see the visible things day after day, like the sun, moon and stars.

We can look all around us and only see the visible things day after day, like the visible sky and clouds.

We can look all around us and only see the visible things day after day, and we are limited to only seeing the visible things because of being born in sin.

We are limited from seeing the invisible things that are unseen to us from day to day, but when God created Adam and Eve so perfect in the Garden of Eden, they both could see the invisible God and talk and walk with Him in the Garden of Eden.

From the very beginning of creation on earth it wasn't meant for human beings to not see the invisible things that became invisible to human beings because of Adam eating that unforbidden fruit from the tree of knowledge, good and evil in the midst of the Garden of Eden.

Adam and Eve's eyes were open to the visible things of sin for disobeying God and their eyes were also closed to seeing the invisible things of God, including not seeing God who became invisible to Adam and Eve because of their sin against Him.

Moses could only hear God talking to Him in a burning bush because Moses was not worthy to look upon God because Moses was born in sin and that limited him to only seeing the visible things.

God had to put a limit on us that only allows us to see the visible things.

God had to put that limit on us to keep us from seeing the invisible things that would scare us because of being born in sin.

Because we have a sinful nature, we would live in fear if we could see the good and evil angels all around us.

We can't even handle all of the visible things that we see because of being born in sin, and God foreknew that before we were born.

God is so merciful to every human being to not let us see the invisible things that would scare us to death if we could see them day after day.

Because we have a sinful nature, we would be afraid of a ghost if it appeared before our eyes on any day or night.

We can only see the visible things from day to day and we can truly thank God for letting us see only the visible things in this world where the fallen angels are invisible to our naked eyes but can appear to us in the visible form of a human being who we are often not afraid to see from day to day.

God is so merciful to not allow you and me to see evil angels with our naked eyes because God foreknew that they would scare us to death because that's what they want to do.

God will not even allow us to see an angel from heaven with our naked eyes.

We can see an unaware angel in a human form that won't scare us because an angel from heaven in the form of a human being wont' scare us but will cause us to feel very comfortable in his presence.

An evil angel can also appear as an angel of light in human form, but will sooner or later cause us to feel very uncomfortable and know that the evil angel in the form of a human being is not about encouraging us to love and keep God's Commandments.

We can only see the visible things, and some visible things can scare us, like seeing a poisonous snake or a hungry lion coming very fast towards us.

The evil invisible things are so much worse and would scare us if we could see them, but God is so merciful to us to not allow us to see them while He protects us from the unseen invisible things.

We are so blessed by God who has limited us to only see the visible things all around us from day to day, while the invisible things all around us can't scare us because God made it to be that way for you and me to come to Him boldly in our prayers unto an invisible all-loving and wise God.

So Pure

Water can flow so pure.

A baby can cry so pure.

A cool breeze can be so pure.

The fruits that grow on a tree are so pure.

A flower can bloom so pure.

Fire can burn so pure.

A bird can fly so pure.

A snake can crawl on the ground so pure.

A dog can wag its tail so pure.

A man can love a woman so pure.

A woman can give birth to a baby so pure.

Someone can have the right motives so pure.

Someone can have good intentions so pure.

The rain can fall down from the clouds in the sky so pure.

The snow can cover the ground so pure.

The leaves can fall from the trees so pure.

The wind can blow so pure.

The ocean waves can splash on the coastal shores so pure.

Someone can be very tired and fall asleep so pure.

Someone can dream so pure.

A child can grow up into an adult so pure.

Someone can smile so pure.

Somone can laugh so pure.

Children can play with one another so pure.

A choice can be made so pure.

Someone can prosper so pure.

Someone can go from rags to riches so pure.

Someone can give a helping hand so pure.

Someone can say something so pure.

Someone can do something so pure.

Someone can think on something so pure.

Someone can age and get old so pure.

A soldier can serve in the military so pure.

A president can serve the nation so pure.

An athlete can win a race so pure.

A ship can sail on the ocean so pure.

A star can fall so pure.

A shadow can move over the landscape so pure.

Someone's body can heal so pure.

Someone can make up for lost time so pure.

Someone can be encouraged so pure.

Someone can be motivated so pure.

Someone can forgive so pure.

A real, true Christian will go to church so pure.

A real, true repentant soul will turn to Jesus so pure.

There is nothing more pure than the fact that God so loved the world that He gave us His only begotten Son so that whosoever believeth in Him shall not perish but shall have eternal life.

The Hardest One to See

The hardest one to see is yourself because your eyes have a hard time seeing your own flaws.

The hardest one to see is yourself, because your eyes have a hard time seeing your mistakes so you can admit to them.

The hardest one to see is yourself, because your eyes have a hard time seeing your own pride.

The hardest one to see is yourself, because your eyes have a hard time seeing your own judgmental ways.

The hardest one to see is yourself, because you have a hard time seeing your own words being hurtful.

The hardest one to see is yourself, because you have a hard time seeing your own words being so wrong to say.

The hardest one to see is yourself, because you can have a hard time hearing your own words being discouraging.

The hardest one to see is yourself, because you can have a hard time hearing your own words being disrespectful.

The hardest one to see is yourself, because you can have a hard time forgiving yourself.

The hardest one to see is yourself, because you can have a hard time seeing your own actions as being stuck up.

The hardest one to see is yourself, because you can have a hard time seeing your own actions as showing favoritism.

The hardest one to see is yourself, because you can have a hard time seeing your own actions as being rude.

The hardest one to see is yourself, because you can have a hard time seeing your own selfish ways.

The hardest one to see is yourself, because you can have a hard time seeing your own sins.

The hardest one to see is yourself, because you can have a hard time seeing the need to change for the better.

The hardest one to see is yourself, because you can have a hard time seeing the need to confess and repent of even one sin that can look so right to hold onto in your own eyes.

The hardest one to see is yourself, because you can have a hard time seeing Jesus speaking to you in His holy word that you can believe doesn't apply to you.

The hardest one to see is yourself, because you think that you know it all but you can't do all things like Jesus.

Only God Has the Right to be God

Only God has the right to be God who is always right about what's in everyone's heart.

Only God has the right to be God who is always right about every thought in everybody's minds.

Only God has the right to be God who is always right about knowing everybody's motives.

Only God has the right to be God who is always right about knowing everybody's intentions.

Only God has the right to be God who is always right about everybody's choices.

Only God has the right to be God who is always right about knowing what everybody will say before they say one word.

Only God has the right to be God who is always right about knowing what everybody will do before they do anything.

Only God has the right to be God who is always right about knowing how long everybody will live.

Only God has the right to be God who is always right about knowing everybody's name.

Only God has the right to be God who is always right about knowing everybody's feelings.

Only God has the right to be God who is always right about giving justice to all who have been treated unfairly.

Only God has the right to be God who is always right about punishing anyone who rebels against Him.

Only God has the right to be God who is always right about knowing anyone who believes in His Son, Jesus Christ.

Only God has the right to be God who is always right about knowing anyone who loves and obeys His Son, Jesus Christ.

Only God has the right to be God who is always right about knowing anyone who is saved in His only begotten Son, Jesus Christ.

Only God has the right to be God who is always and forever right to know that His Son, Jesus Christ, and the Holy Spirit are One with Him in the Trinity Godhead.

Only God has the right to be God who is always right about knowing why He is God.

Only God has the right to be God who is always and eternally right to sit on His holy throne above all existence in heaven and below the heavens.

Only God has the eternal right to be an everlasting, holy and righteous God who is always and infinitely right about not always allowing bad things to happen to all who deny themselves and pick up their crosses to follow His Son, Jesus Christ.

Only God has the right to be God who is always right about knowing what choices you and I will make before we make any choice.

Only God has every right to be God who is always right about knowing without any surprises who will enter into heaven with His Son, Jesus Christ, when He comes back again on the clouds of glory.

Only God has full rights to be God who is always right about knowing who will be surprised to see someone in heaven who they believed to have been lost in their sins.

The Lord Can

The winter's cold ice can cover over the grass, trees and fields and make them look like a work of art, but not the artwork created by any human being.

The spring's warmth can cause the birds to sing and the flowers to bloom and draw the bees to them.

The fall's cool breeze can slow us down whenever we go here and there feeling somewhat at ease about many things that we have no control over from day to day.

The summer's heat can energize us to want to do a lot of things as if we can't get tired and need no rest like the water flowing in the river.

A day can go by so fast that it causes us not to remember everything that we did.

A week can seem to move so slowly to us who can want to do things so fast.

A month can seem to look at us in our eyes and say to us, "I am not moving on."

A year can change us in ways that we don't see coming.

An hour can seem to be like a very long time if we are in trouble that we did not cause.

A minute can seem like forever if our life is in great danger and we don't know when we will be out of that danger.

One second can cause us to freeze up and not know what to say or do if death is rushing very fast to take our breath away from us so unexpectedly.

The Lord can work out everything in our lives while we are sleeping in our beds at night, not knowing anything that is going on around us.

The Lord sees all things and knows all things before we were born, and the Lord was making His plans to back up our bad choices to not be greater than His grace for us to repent and turn to Him before it's too late.

Not Always Peaches and Cream

The Christian parents in the church need to let their children know that living for Jesus is not always peaches and cream that tastes good.

The Christian parents need to teach their children that this Christian journey can be a hard road to walk down because there is a devil who hates every child of God no matter what age they are.

Loving Jesus and keeping His Commandments will not always be peaches and cream that many people love to eat because it's a very tasty dessert to want to eat after a good meal.

Every Christian needs to stay focused and know that we will be tried and tested through our trials for Jesus' holy name sake, and the children of Christian parents are not exempted from going through some hardships for Jesus' name sake.

The Christian parents in the church need to prepare their children for their wilderness journey that they will walk through for Jesus' holy name sake.

If any Christian causes their child or children to believe that having a relationship with Jesus will always be peaches and cream, then they are setting up their child or children to be greatly disappointed.

Jesus, Himself, was always in a very good relationship with His heavenly Father God, but there was a time that came for Jesus to decide whether to not drink of the cup of God's wrath or drink of the cup of God's wrath that was not peaches and cream for Jesus.

Christian parents in the church need to always teach their child or children about the facts of Christian living that has ups and downs, and no Christian parents should deny that truth before their child or children so as not to handicap them spiritually.

If any Christian parents cause their child or children to believe that this Christian walk with Jesus will always be peaches and cream, then they are enemies to their child or children and most of all they are enemies to Jesus whose life wasn't always peaches and cream when He lived in this rotten, sinful world.

Even When Things are Not Going Well

Even when things are not going well in my life, You, O Lord, are still so good to me to allow me to live through the things that are not going well in my life.

Your goodness will overshadow the bad days that only You, O Lord, can make to shine before others to be my testimony about You, O Lord, bringing me safely through my bad days.

Even when things are not going well in my life, O Lord, Your mercy on me makes my life abundant in my hardships that are only temporary compared to Your mercies made new upon me day after day.

Your forgiveness upon me is like a beautiful, sunny sky hovering over me to energize my soul to go to new spiritual heights in You, my Lord, when You bring me out of the things that are not good in my life that I brought upon myself.

Even when things are not going so well in my life, O Lord, You are the miracle worker to give me the strength to bear my troubles and You will remove them from me on your perfect time for me and others to see Your power overpowering the devil and making him flee from me to enter into Your holy tabernacle and give You, O Lord, all the glory and praise on Your holy Sabbath day of rest that is a good thing for everyone to worship You in spirit and truth, O Lord.

This Life is Nothing Good Compared To

This life is nothing good compared to the eternal life that Jesus Christ will give to you and me for being saved in Him.

You and I don't know what living is until Jesus Christ comes back again to take us to heaven where living is eternal in Jesus Christ.

The worst life that anyone can live in this sinful world is a bad life that is short-lived under the sun compared to the eternal life beyond the sun where the least in heaven are living a glorious life in Jesus Christ.

Life in this sinful world is full of uncertainty and ups and downs that you and I have become so numb to that we can believe that life was meant to be like playing Russian roulette.

We Christians believe that there is an eternal life in Jesus Christ who we believe to be true and faithful to His holy word telling us about Jesus Christ who is the ternal life beyond life here on earth.

This life that we live in our mortal bodes yearns for the eternal life that even unbelievers portray in big screen movies showing afterlife scenes of having an immortal body full of power and victory over death that couldn't keep them in the grave.

Only Jesus Christ has made that accomplishment of having victory over the grave and death that movie performers can't ever do even though they can make billions of dollars from viewers being so caught up in their performances on the big movie screens.

This life is nothing good at all compared to the eternal life that the fallen angels truly know was something so miraculous after they gave it up and now regret it forever and ever.

They truly know what every Christian will greatly receive for believing in Jesus Christ who is the eternal life that no one else can compare to.

Regardless Of

Regardless of the lack of love in the church, I will grow stronger in You, my Lord, just by going to church that you, my Lord Jesus Christ, are the head of and I will keep my eyes fixed on You.

Regardless of the favoritism in the church, I know that You love me, my Lord, with an everlasting love having no respect of persons.

Regardless of the tares in the church, I can always go to church with You, my Lord, in my heart and no tares will come between me and You, my Lord Jesus Christ.

Regardless of who are not blessed by my spiritual gifts in the church, no one can take away Your Holy Spirit from dwelling in me to be a blessing to someone in the church.

Regardless of who leaves the church, I can put my trust in You, my Lord Jesus, who will never leave me or forsake me because no one and nothing can take You, my Lord, away from me.

Regardless of the trials I go through, only You, my Lord, can number my days in the church that belongs to You to add many more years to my life for me to assemble myself together with my brothers and sisters in the church.

Regardless of who doesn't love me in the church and outside the church, You , my Lord, have called me to be in Your church to worship You in spirit and truth that no one can take away from me because of You, my Lord, giving me a free will to choose You over any human being who doesn't know what love is without loving You, my Lord and Savior Jesus Christ.

Regardless of me being so messed up in imperfection, even in the church, I can confess my sins to You, my Lord, who will cleanse me of my sins so they don't rub off on anyone in the church and outside the church where You, my Lord, can work in mysterious ways to help me to change someone's life to want to seek You out more and more.

Regardless of me falling short of God's glory, You, my Lord, will not cast me out of Your church for as long as I love You and keep Your Commandments that Your Holy Spirit will help me to keep one day at a time.

Regardless of the people of the world and so-called Christians who only pretend to be like You, my Lord, I can choose to deny myself and pick up my cross and follow You inside the church and outside the church where only You, my Lord, know all who are in Your sheep fold that has no one to be a mistake even in the last hour to repent and turn to You before it's too late.

Only You, my Lord, know the too late fate being upon anyone regardless of them being in the church all of their lives or never being in the church like the thief on the cross who asked You to remember him in his last hour.

Regardless of who believes that he or she knows they are saved in You, O Lord, or not saved in You, my Lord, only You are the head of the church to judge everyone in all of Your righteousness and fairness that no one else is worthy to have in this world regardless of what office someone has in the church and outside the church.

Regardless of walking by and driving by the church and seeing proof of people going in the church, whether they are Christians or hypocrites, it's never wise to keep putting Jesus off as if you have all the time in the world to come to Jesus.

Waiting until the last hour doesn't always work for anyone, regardless of repenting that may be too late to turn to Jesus because of having no true repentance and turning to Him out of fear and not true surrender unto Jesus.

Regardless of pretense church folks, the church will still do a lot of good to you and me for keeping our eyes fixed on Jesus Christ who is the head of the church to even shake up some pretense church folks to get real about repenting and turning to Him so He does not shake them out of the church.

Regardless of you and me being real about Jesus, we are not exempted from any hard times in life that the wicked and the righteous will have in life.

But only the righteous know what it means to put one's hope and trust in Jesus Christ to stand on His promises that no hard times can ever crush.

Rejection Can Be a Blessing from the Lord

Rejection can be a blessing from the Lord to spare you and me suffering and pain down the road of life.

Rejection can be a blessing from the Lord who truly sees that woman who you truly like as that woman rejects you, but the Lord knows that she is not the right woman for you.

That doesn't make her bad, she is just the right woman for another man.

Rejection can be a blessing from the Lord, even when you and I can be rejected by someone who doesn't want what we give to them and makes us feel bad.

When you and I get rejected by someone who doesn't want to hear anything about Jesus, the devil will use our rejection for our bad but Jesus can use it for our good as we brush the dust off of our feet and go to someone else who the Lord knows will listen to us and be blessed by us for uplifting Jesus' holy name before them.

Rejection is not a completely bad thing; it can be a blessing from the Lord to make us stronger and more determined to win souls to be saved in Jesus Christ.

The Lord will allow you and me to be rejected from time to time to let us know that He was rejected by many people who just didn't want to believe in him, but Jesus still loved them and wanted to save them from their sins.

Rejection can be a blessing from the Lord because there are folks, especially church folks, who got rejected by the opposite sex and truly thank Jesus for protecting them from marrying someone who was not right for them.

Being rejected has saved many people's lives from a very bad heartache that would have killed them.

Being rejected has also saved you and me who the Lord protected with rejection that ended up being a blessing to us.

We can truly thank the Lord today for still being alive to know that rejection is a good thing if the Lord is in it.

We may not see this until many years later, but eventually we will realize that us being rejected by them was for our good today.

Physically Sick
and Spiritually Sick

When we are physically sick, we know that we are sick because we feel bad.

When we are physically sick, we know that we want to get well so that we can do the things we normally do from day to day.

When we get physically sick, we know that we are not our true selves and we really can't do much of anything.

When we are physically sick, we don't usually feel like talking and we usually don't want to go anywhere.

When we are physically sick, we usually don't feel like having any company over to our house and we usually don't' feel like getting up out of bed.

We know that a physical sickness can surely get the best of us to the point that we don't even feel like getting down on our knees and praying to the Lord.

A physical sickness can surely cause us to not feel like reading our bible.

Everybody, whether they're good or evil, dislikes being physically sick, which can make us all feel so bad until we get well.

Many people are spiritually sick and don't feel bad about rejecting Jesus Christ.

Many people are spiritually sick and feel good about living in their sins.

Many people are spiritually sick and don't care about wanting to get spiritually well in Jesus Christ.

Many people are spiritually sick and don't know that they are spiritually unwell because they don't believe in Jesus Christ who is the only One to make us all spiritually well.

The difference between being physically sick and spiritually sick is that everybody knows when they are physically sick but everybody doesn't know that they are spiritually sick and need to repent and turn to Jesus, who can make our sin-sick soul well in Him.

The difference between being physically sick and spiritually sick is that being physically sick can take us to the grave, but being spiritually sick can take us to an eternal death for not loving Jesus and keeping His Commandments.

Love

It's easy to love people who will encourage you and me.

It's hard to love people who will discourage you and me.

It's easy to love people who will accept you and me for who we are.

It's hard to love people who will act like they are better than you and me.

It's easy to love people who will talk nice to you and me.

It's hard to love people who will talk mean to you and me.

It's easy to love people who won't change on you and me.

It's hard to love people who will change on you and me.

It's easy to love people who will rejoice with you and me for making a good achievement.

It's hard to love people who have no joy for you and me making a good achievement

It's easy to love people who will treat you and me right.

It's hard to love people who will treat you and me wrong.

It's easy to love people who will agree with you and me.

It's hard to love people who will disagree with you and me.

It's easy to love people who will help you and me.

It's hard to love people who won't help you and me.

It's easy to love people who will tell you and me the truth.

It's hard to love people who will tell you and me a lie.

It's easy to love people who are real with you and me.

It's hard to love people who are so phony to you and me.

It's easy to love people who are good at saying all the right words.

It's hard to love people who are not good at saying all the right words.

It's easy to love people who want the best for you and me

It's hard to love people who don't care to want the best for you and me.

It's easy to love people who are on our side.

It's hard to love people who are against you and me.

It's easy to love people who are a good friend to you and me.

It's hard to love people who don't care about being a good friend to you and me.

It's easy to love people who will not use you and me.

It's hard to love people who will use you and me.

It's easy to love people who don't act like they are better than you and me.

It's hard to love people who are proud and arrogant.

It's easy to love people who will look in your eyes and my eyes when they talk to you and me.

It's hard to love people who won't look in your eyes and my eyes when they talk to you and me.

It's easy to love people who you and I trust.

It's hard to love people who you and I don't trust.

It's easy to love people who will smile at you and me.

It's hard to love people who will never smile at you and me.

It's easy to love people who love you and me.

It's hard to love people who don't love you and me.

It's easy to love church folks who get up out of their church pew and give you and me a hug or handshake.

It's hard to love church folks who make no effort to get up out of the church pew to give you and me a hug or handshake to show you and me some love.

It's easy to love church folks who love you and me.

It's hard to love church folks who walk through the church doors and enter in to the sanctuary as if you and I are not there and they do not even look at you and me or speak to you and me sitting in the pew as they enter the church.

It's easy to love church folks who will give you and me a warm meal to eat after the church service is over.

It's hard to love church folks who don't look happy about giving you and me a warm meal after the church service is over.

It's easy to love church folks who love you and me.

It's hard to love church folks who will keep their distance from you and me in their body language that speaks louder than their words of love.

It's easy to love the Lord as long as the Lord will answer our prayers.

It's hard to love the Lord when the Lord doesn't answer our prayers on our time.

It's easy to love the Lord as long as the Lord gives you and me His blessings.

It's hard to love the Lord when the Lord allows hardships to come upon you and me who can believe that we're supposed to have it easy in life because we are Christians.

It's easy to love the Lord Jesus Christ as long as the Lord blesses your health and my health.

It's hard to love the Lord Jesus Christ if the Lord allows you and me to get very sick and feel like the Lord has abandoned you and me.

Job must've felt like God had abandoned him too, which made him question God who said to Job, "Where were you when I laid down the foundations of the earth?"

At that time, it was hard for Job's wife to love God because she asked Job to curse God and die, and there was no love in her words for God who still loved her as well as Job and blessed them with more wealth than what they had before in the past.

It's easy for the Lord to love you and me, even when we don't' love Him in ways that you and I don't see.

It's hard for the Lord to love anyone who rejects His Holy Spirit teaching us all truth about God who hates all sin.

God is love, but it doesn't mean that it's always easy for God to love us, especially if we make it a practice to live in our sins against Him.

God love us, but God is no fool and will not let anyone enter into heaven with their unconfessed and unrepentant sins.

God hates that and it can make it hard for God to love us if we don't believe in His Son, Jesus Christ, who is forever easy for God to love.

It can be hard for God to always love you and me who can take God's love for us to be weak and believe that we can make excuses for sinning against Him.

Doing that can make it hard for God to love us, especially when we can choose to make it easy for God to love us if we love Him.

There is no scripture in the bible that says it's always easy for God to love you and me who can make it hard for God to always love us.

There was a time when Got regretted that He made man and it looked like it became hard for God to love rebellious people, until God found favor in Noah.

You and I can make it hard for the Lord God and Savior Jesus Christ to love us, but at the same time, Jesus loves us enough to save us from our sins that He hates, but He doesn't hate us.

You and I can make it hard for the Lord to love us, but at the same time, the Lord will never hate our souls.

That's what the devil hates and he tried his best to cause God to hate that he made man, but he failed because of Jesus Christ who redeemed man back to God on Mount Calvery.

Back in the bible days, it was easy for Jesus to love people who loved Him and followed Him wherever He went as He shared the love of God, His heavenly Father.

It was hard for Jesus to love the Pharisees who Jesus called a brood of vipers for speaking evil against the good that He did.

Jesus loved the Pharisees' souls and wanted to save them from their sins that He hated.

Even though the Pharisees made it hard for Jesus to love them and He had to always be on His guard against them whenever they approached him with words of trickery, Jesus saw right through them and still loved them.

It wasn't easy for Jesus to love the Pharisees and religious leaders who He called hypocrites and gave them no loving words.

Jesus hated no one and loved everyone's souls so much that He gave up His life on the cross to save them from being lost in sin.

If there were people who were hard for Jesus to love back in the bible days, when Jesus lived among many sinners, then it will be hard for you and me to love even hypocrites in the church — but we have to love them like Jesus loved them while we hate their sins.

If we love sin, then we surely don't love Jesus, because no one can love living in their sins and love Jesus at the same time.

Loving Jesus is easy for a real, true Christian who is born again in the spirit of God and has been baptized down under the water to come back up out of the water as a new creature in Jesus Christ.

If you and I have a hard time loving Jesus, then we haven't been born again in the Holy Spirit of God and have no newness of life, no matter how long we've been in the church.

The devil can be in the church for a long time.

Loving Jesus is easy for anyone who keeps his or her eyes fixed on Jesus on good and bad days.

If it's hard for us to love Jesus, then there is no real love for Jesus in you and me.

It will be easy for us to love one another if we love Jesus.

Will Go On

The day will go on into the night while we can get stuck holding a grudge.

The night will go on into the day while we can get stuck in telling a lie.

The sun will go on shining all day while we can get stuck in showing respect of persons.

The moon will glow all night while we can get stuck in our pride.

The stars will sparkle all night while we can get stuck in seeking revenge.

The wind will go on blowing while we can get stuck in only being full of hot air.

The trees will go on standing tall while we can get stuck in gossiping.

The grass will go on covering the ground while we can get stuck in backbiting.

The ground will go on being under our feet while we can get stuck in being selfish.

The seasons will go on changing while we can get stuck in holding onto unconfessed sins.

The bible will go on being holy while we can get stuck in not living a holy life.

The ten Commandments will go on being the law of God while we can get stuck in breaking the ten Commandments.

The church will go on being the bride of Jesus Christ while we can get stuck in committing spiritual adultery.

Jesus Christ will go on being the head of the church while we can get stuck in being the tail and not the head in representing Jesus Christ before unbelievers.

Jesus Christ will go on being the Savior of the world while we can get stuck in being spiritually lukewarm.

The Christian journey will go on with having hardships for Jesus' holy name sake while we can get stuck in believing that the fiery dots thrown at us is something strange on our Christian journey.

Salvation in Jesus Christ will go on until God closes His probation on this sinful world while we can get stuck in judging one another to be wheat or tare that only Jesus can judge and separate.

Jesus will go on saving repentant souls to go to heaven with Him when He comes back again on the clouds of glory, while we can get stuck in believing that we have all the time in this world to get it right with Jesus.

We are No Match for the Devil

We are no match for the devil who would destroy us all if Jesus was dead in the grave that had no power to keep Jesus down in the grave.

Many people, even in the church, just don't know how evil the devil really is; he is much more evil than Hitler was with his genocide.

Many people, even in the church, speak the devil's name too lightly as if they have the power to cause the devil to flee from them.

We are no match for the devil who would kill us even in a dream if Jesus was not there in our dreams to rescue us from the devil.

The devil is much more evil than cannibalism, but many people, even in the church, look at the devil like he can't do anything evil to them.

We are no match for the devil without Jesus being on our side to give us the victory over the devil and make him flee from us.

The devil is much more evil than death that would relieve us of life's hardships, but being alive and tormented by the devil is worse than death.

Many people, even in the church, look at the devil as being powerless because they believe they're so strong in Jesus, until the devil strikes them down with a deadly sickness.

We are no match for the devil who Job was no match for as well as his wife, who told Job to curse God and die.

The devil would have taken Job's life if God had allowed it, but God didn't let the devil take Job's life.

It was the devil who killed all of Job's children because the devil is nothing but evil every day.

The devil would kill you and me dead if Jesus allowed him to do so.

We are no match for the devil who is much more evil than all the manmade horror movies that come nowhere close to the real devil who hates God.

He arranged the death of Jesus Christ, who God rose from the grave to kill the devil in fire and brimstone one day.

We are no match for the devil who many people, even in the church, play on his evil playground that has nothing but spiritual landmines to blow up our souls so they'll be lost in his darkness of sins.

We are no match for the devil who many people don't believe exists, but those same people will blame God for their misfortunes that were brought upon them by the devil because he wants them to curse God.

Spiritual Things
are the Best Blessings

Spiritual things are the best blessings from the Lord because spiritual things have no erosions.

Spiritual things are the best blessings from the Lord because spiritual things have no breakdowns.

Spiritual things are the best blessings from the Lord because spiritual things have no rust and will not wear away.

Spiritual things are the best blessings from the Lord because spiritual things have no rust or stains.

Spiritual things are the best blessings from the Lord because spiritual things have no mold or mildew.

Spiritual things are the best blessings from the Lord because spiritual things have no deterioration.

Spiritual things are the best blessings from the Lord because spiritual things have no fading.

Spiritual things are the best blessings from the Lord because spiritual things have no problems.

Spiritual things are the best blessings from the Lord because spiritual things have no temporal existence.

Spiritual things are the best blessings from the Lord because spiritual things have no passing away.

Material things can surely pass away — that's been proven by time that the Lord created for you and me to live for Him before our time runs out.

Time has proven that spiritual things are the very best blessings that we can always hold onto and never regret it, but we can regret having some material things that can break down on us and need repair work while we are still paying on them.

No One Can Escape from Time

It's just a matter of time before a criminal will get caught.

It's just a matter of time before a dedicated college student will graduate from college.

No one can escape from time.

In due time, the seasons do change.

In due time, we reap what we sow.

No one can escape from time.

It's just a matter of time before a secret will be revealed.

It's just a matter of time before a pretender will be found out for who he or she really is.

No one can escape from time.

In due time, a foolish man and woman will be trouble to even their own household.

In due time, a wise man and woman will be favored over a fool.

No one can escape from time.

It's just a matter of time before every Christian will go through some kind of trial for Jesus' holy name sake.

It's just a matter of time before every Christian must examine themselves to be true to Jesus, even on their worst day.

No one can escape from time that only exists under the sun where everybody in this world needs some time to know who they really are before God, who gives everybody borrowed time that a fool will believe he or she can escape from and make it to heaven without believing in Jesus Christ.

Jesus came to this world in the fullness of time for no one who ever lived and is still alive today can escape from under the sun where Jesus fulfilled everyone's time for everyone to love God and keep His commandments from the beginning to the end of this world where no one can escape from time that is a gift to us from God.

Who can escape from time under the sun where Jesus lived on time that He created to come into this world in the fullness of time to be the Light of the world?

Jesus could not escape from the time that He would give up His life on the cross to save all men from their sins.

Jesus rose from the grave on time with the victory over death and the grave.

No one can escape from time because we are only here on earth and not in heaven and the unfallen worlds where time doesn't exist because only eternity exists there.

Time is necessary for only sinners like you and me who are living on borrowed time for us to be saved in Jesus Christ before time runs out of God's saving grace.

Life Will Not Always Be Easy

Life will not always be easy, but it's always good to do what the Lord tell us to do.

If the Lord makes it hard on us, then it is for our good for the Lord to save us from being lost in our sins.

Life will not always be easy, but it's always good to love and obey the Lord who says that it's better to suffer for living unto Him than to suffer for living unto the devil who wants us all to be lost in our sins.

Life will not always be easy, but we can be joyful in the Lord because Jesus overcame the world to not overpower us with its troubles, and Jesus will not allow the devil to tempt us with more than we can handle from day to day.

Life will not always be easy, especially for every true child of God, but we can make our calling very sure in Jesus Christ through our prayers, bible studies and most of all just believing in Jesus Christ to be our Lord and Savior who gives us the strength to keep our eyes fixed on Him.

Life will not always be easy for us born again believers in Jesus Christ, whose life wasn't always easy when He lived in this sinful world among nothing but imperfect people who had sins to confess and repent unto Him who had no sins in His flesh.

Life will not always be easy for anyone to live in this fallen world where life is also hard on unbelievers who the devil can easily possess to live in their sins, day after day, with no guilt or shame before the Lord Jesus Christ.

Life will not always be easy, but the creator of all life is Jesus Christ, who will give us an abundant life for loving Him and keeping His Commandments that will not be a burden for anyone to keep if we love Jesus who made it easy for all men to be saved in Him because He gave up his life on a hard cross with hard, sharp nails being driven through His hands and feet.

That was nothing easy for Jesus to bear to save us from being lost in our sins.

Life will not always be easy for you and me, especially when we deny ourselves and pick up our crosses to follow Jesus Christ day after day.

We need the Holy Spirit to make us very aware that living for Jesus will not always be easy, even in the church where the pretenders can surely make it hard on you and me.

Life will not always be easy for anyone in the church and outside the church, but Jesus made a promise to give eternal life to anyone who believes in Him.

This just shows that Jesus has given everyone borrowed time to be saved in Him before it's too late.

Life will not always be easy for anyone in this world, but on judgement day no one can say that God was not fair to them and didn't give them a choice to repent and turn to Jesus who made that easy for everyone to do through God's grace that is sufficient for the uttermost sinners to be saved in Jesus Christ.

Up in Heaven

Up in heaven there will be no white people living on one side of heaven and no black people living on another side of heaven.

Up in heaven there will be no Asian people living on one side of heaven and no Latino people living on another side of heaven.

Up in heaven there will be no white people living on the north side of heaven and no black people living on the east side of heaven.

Up in heaven there will be no Asian people living on the south side of heaven and no Latino people living on the west side of heaven.

Up in heaven there will be no prejudice, no discrimination and no segregation because up in heaven there will be nothing but love that everyone will have for one another throughout the heavens.

So many people want to go to heaven where there is nothing but love, but while they live on earth they will hate many people they see who don't look like them.

Loving everybody, no matter the color of their skin, starts here on earth, just like it will be when we one day go back to heaven with Jesus Christ when He comes back again to raise the righteous dead in every skin color to join the righteous living in every skin color to go to heaven.

Up in heaven there will be every kind of nationality of people and tribe of people who love Jesus and love their neighbors, who is everybody in this world who God loves so much, regardless of the color of their skin.

Up in heaven there will be nothing but unity, and all the holy saints will see no color of the skin and it will be like that throughout the heavens where no evils of hatred will exist before God.

Lucifer and his angels were cast out of heaven because of their hatred towards God, who will not accept any kind of prejudice or discrimination or segregation up in heaven.

Many people want to go to heaven, but will make many people's lives a living hell because they don't look like them and have the same skin color.

Jesus never had a problem with this when He lived in this world without sin in His flesh to save us from our sins.

There are many prejudiced people in every skin color below the heavens, but up in heaven only the righteous will live there because they treated everybody right and fair, no matter the color of their skin.

Up in heaven there will be every color of skin and all people will love one another throughout eternity when Jesus comes back again on the clouds of glory to take all of his children with Him to heaven where no color of the skin will be a threat to anyone.

Everybody is Important to Jesus

Everybody is important to Jesus who loves everybody all the same way each and every day that nobody is unimportant to Jesus.

We live in a world where many people are being worshipped and put above the poor because they are so wealthy and think they are worthy to look down on anyone who is less fortunate than they are.

Many people in this world are so very highly intelligent and will be put up on a high pedestal in the eyes of their admirers, but everybody is important to Jesus no matter how unintelligent they may be.

Jesus doesn't have a problem with anyone's disabilities; they are unimportant to Jesus who can use anyone to build up His church that is made up of all kinds of broken people from all walks of life.

Everybody is so very important to Jesus who gave up His life on the cross to save everybody, great and small, from their sins.

Jesus doesn't have a problem with anyone being poor, middle class, upper middle class or rich because everybody's soul is important for Jesus to save from being lost in sin.

The status quo is unimportant to Jesus, who shows no favoritism to use even those who are uneducated because no one can educate anyone better than the Holy Spirit who teaches all the truth and provides the greatest education that anyone can ever get.

Everybody is important to Jesus who leaves no one out of His saving grace, even though many people, even in the church, will leave out whoever they see to be of no importance.

They won't even look at those they deem as unimportant as they enter into the church, as if they are the only ones who can be important to Jesus.

Everybody is important to Jesus who the devil is no match for to be one day cast into fire and brimstone.

Everybody is important to Jesus, no matter how unimportant you and I are to especially selfish people who feel so important in their own eyes but are spiritually blind to Jesus.

The Days Were Created on Earth

The days were created on earth, not in the heavens that God created before He created the earth.

The bible says that God created the heavens and the earth.

It seems to be that God created the heavens first, and that may have been trillions of light years before He created earth.

Could that word "and" mean that the heavens and earth weren't created at the same exact time because there were no days created in the heavens, only hear on earth?

That word "and" between the heavens and earth may be trillions of light years between when God created the earth after He created the heavens where no number of days exist — that's only here on earth where the first day right on down to the seventh day were created by God who created everything in the earth in six days and He rested from all of His works on the seventh day.

If God didn't create any days in the heavens, then is it possible that the angels and creatures in the unfallen worlds don't have to keep the Holy Sabbath day of rest that God created for man to rest from all of his works that God gave to man to do in six days?

God created the days here on earth even before this world had fallen into sin that breaks God's perfect, holy and righteous law that God gave to all human beings to keep.

It looks to be that God only created the days to be only on earth where the first day began as God created the days down to the seventh day that God said to remember to keep holy.

If God created the Sabbath for the holy angels in heaven to keep, then the angels would have to rest from their works of protecting you and me from the unfallen evil angels on the seventh day.

If this was the case, the unfallen angels would possess us all for having no guardian angels to protect us.

No angel in heaven would come to our rescue because of resting from all their works on the seventh day.

God is a perfect, holy and righteous all-wise God who foreknew that no days would be needed in the heavens, only here on earth where God created man to be a little lower than the angels.

God had no need to create any days in the heavens for the angels and the unfallen worlds to live under and they would need no rest on the seventh day and God really didn't need to rest from all of His creation either.

God is an eternal God who never gets tired because God is a spirit and not flesh and blood like you and I are made of so that we get tired and need to rest on God's holy Sabbath day of rest.

The devil is an evil spirit who never gets tired of tempting you and me to sin against God seven days a week.

God forever foreknew that many people here on earth would take the days for granted, as if any day is their slave to do what they tell the days to do.

Only God has the power to tell the days what to bring to us because the days will bow down to worship God who only created the days to be here on earth for our good to pass God's test if not one day, then hopefully another day that we can only live one day at a time.

The days were created here on earth after God created the heavens where the days didn't begin for the angels and unfallen worlds to have a birthday to celebrate or an anniversary or holiday to celebrate or a holy Sabbath day of rest in the heavens.

There are no days in heaven that is eternal to have no days, weeks, months, years, decades and no centuries to exist because of God's Son, Jesus Christ, creating the heavens eternal and He will one day make us eternal like a day never existed to be our birthday.

Is it so wrong to speculate about anything that might have some truth to it?

Jesus will reveal His eternal truth to us when He comes back again to take us to heaven if we are saved in Him.

The truth that we get from the bible is only a small thing compared to the endless creations of God that eternity can't keep up with.

The days were created on earth like the bible says in the book of Genesis that says nothing about the first day down to the seventh day being created in heaven.

There are bible geniuses who say that there are three heavens.

The first heaven is where God is sitting on His holy throne in the presence of all the holy angels.

The second heaven is the universe that only the Lord knows where it begins and ends.

The third heaven is the sky high above the earth.

It seems to be that God created the days only here on earth where the days have a fixed cycle to change in the exact order that God created the days to do from the first day down to the seventh day that God made to be holy for all men to rest from all of their labors.

There are no days in heaven that are not mentioned in the bible that says that God is the ancient of days but the ancient of days are eternal to have no number to them like our days do, because our days are numbered in sin that the first Adam brought upon us all great and small.

If there were days in the heavens then there would be nights in the heavens because God created the days to turn into the nights that we can only see here on earth.

The Good Guys to Win

In a war movie, many movie watchers want the good guys to win the war, even if many movie makers don't believe in Jesus Christ who was the good guy who came down from heaven and was born in a manger.

In a horror movie, many movie watchers want the good guys to win at the end of the movie.

Many horror movie watchers don't read the bible that tells us about Jesus casting out demons that possessed many people and made things like a horror movie.

In a romance movie, many movie watchers want the good guys to get the good women at the end of the movie.

Many romance movie watchers don't read the bible that tells us about Jesus Christ who loves His church bride so much that He is coming back again to take His bride to heaven and away from that bad guy called the devil who is full of lies that he loves to tell to Jesus' church bride to try to cause the church to stray away from Jesus.

Hollywood will usually produce movies where the good guys win because the good guys always have good hearts and want to do good things for their fellow man so everyone can live in peace instead of strife.

If Hollywood can see that is right for the good guys to win in the end, then what about God who is good all the time to you and me?

God sent a good guy to this world to save us from our sins that originated from a bad guy called the devil who is so bad all the time and would devour you and me if that good guy, Jesus Christ, didn't give up His life on the cross to pay our price.

That good guy, Jesus Christ, rose from the grave with the victory over death and the grave to give you and me His free gift of eternal life when He comes back again on the clouds of glory.

No Hollywood movie can top that with all the good guys that win at the end of the movies.

It just goes to show that the origin of all the good guys is Jesus Christ, who the bad guys can't defeat.

That bad guy called the devil knows too well that he was no match for Jesus up in heaven.

Jesus cast the devil out of heaven with one third of the angels who are bad all the time and try to tempt you and me to do bad things.

If a good guy in a Hollywood movie was defeated, surely many movie watchers will feel that pain because they wanted the good guy to win.

The movie good guy represents the good they have in their hearts, whether they are a Christian or not a Christian.

No good guy will ever be more good than Jesus Christ, and we just can't imagine how good He is to lay some people down in the grave for their good to be saved in Jesus before He stands up and says that it is finished.

The righteous will remain righteous and the wicked will remain wicked and the good guy, Jesus Christ, will show all the angels and all the unfallen worlds that He is a good judge and will be fair to all mankind from the beginning to the end of this world.

What Good Is

What good is a candle without a flame?

What good is a frame without a picture in the frame?

What good is a fan without blades?

What good is a clock without its second hand?

What good is a chair without a seat?

What good is a dinner table without any spates, spoons, forks and napkins on it?

What good is a loveseat without any lovers sitting down together on it?

What good is a door without a lock?

What good is a window without anyone looking out it?

What good is a fireplace without a fire burning in it?

What good is a chimney without any smoke coming out of it?

What good is a vase without any flowers in it?

What good is a refrigerator without any food in it?

What good is a lamp without a lightbulb?

What good is a closet without clothes and shoes in it?

What good is a bed without anyone laying down to sleep in it?

What good is a bathtub without anyone taking a bath in it?

What good is a vacuum cleaner without anyone to vacuum the carpet?

What good is an oven without anyone baking any food in it?

What good is a toaster without anyone toasting bread, waffles and bagels in it?

What good is a microwave without anyone heating up their food in it?

What good is a house without anyone living in it?

What good is a car without anyone driving it?

What good is an airplane without anyone flying it?

What good is a ship without anyone steering it?

What good is an education without anyone learning anything?

What good is a television without anyone turning it on and watching it?

What good is a sermon without anyone in the church to hear it?

What good is teaching without any students?

What good is getting married without marrying your true love?

What good is the church without Jesus Christ being the head of it?

What good is going to church without having love for one another?

What good is getting baptized without the Holy Spirit changing your life for you to live for Jesus?

What good is being a minister without having a relationship with Jesus Christ?

What good is having spiritual gifts in the church without humbling ourselves unto Jesus Christ?

What good are you and I without loving Jesus and keeping His Commandments?

What good is a mirror without anyone looking into it?

The mirror of God's holy law is the best mirror that everyone can look into because it's the only mirror to show us our sins that we need to see to be good for us to repent and lived for Jesus, which we can only do one day at a time.

What good is even being alive without being filled with the Holy Spirit who makes us spiritually alive to live for Jesus?

We would be spiritually dead without Jesus in our lives.

Jesus is Our Only Guarantee

There is no guarantee for our mail to get to its destination.

There is no guarantee we will not get in a car accident on the road.

There is no guarantee to even wake up in the morning.

Jesus is our only guarantee to give us life, health and strength.

There is no guarantee that anyone won't live in an illusion and die in an illusion.

There is no guarantee we will say the right words all the time.

There is no guarantee we will always have the right motives.

Jesus is our only guarantee to help us to make the right choices.

There is no guarantee we will always stay focused on anything.

There is no guarantee we will always do the right thing.

There is no guarantee we will make all the right friends.

Jesus is our only guarantee to always be our best friend.

There is no guarantee that someone won't make you and me angry.

There is no guarantee that everyone will learn from their mistakes.

There is no guarantee that your children will not get into any trouble.

Jesus is our only guarantee to always love us through the thick and thin.

There is no guarantee we will never get sick.

There is no guarantee we will never get lost.

There is no guarantee we will find what we lost.

Jesus is our only guarantee to find us and bring us back to His holy word to live by.

There is no guarantee in money.

There is no guarantee in food.

There is no guarantee in the clothes we wear.

Jesus is our only guarantee to always be there for us, even if we don't feel His presence.

There is no guarantee in knowledge.

There is no guarantee in technology.

There is no guarantee in science.

Jesus is our only guarantee if we believe in Him to be saved.

There is no guarantee in our vehicle.

There is no guarantee in our house.

There is no guarantee in our pets.

Jesus is our only guarantee so we can always depend on Him.

There is no guarantee in a job.

There is no guarantee in the government.

There is no guarantee in our nation.

Jesus is our only guarantee to provide for all of our needs.

There is no guarantee in ourselves.

There is no guarantee in anything that we have.

There is no guarantee in material things.

Jesus is our only guarantee so we can put all of our trust in Him day after day.

There is no guarantee in any human being.

There is no guarantee in the best of our intentions.

There is no guarantee in anything in this world.

Jesus is our only real, true guarantee to make us right before God through His righteousness.

There is no guarantee that everyone in the church is like Jesus.

There is no guarantee that our spiritual gifts will bless everyone in the church.

There is no guarantee that everyone in the church will love you and me.

Jesus is our only guarantee to always love us, inside the church and outside the church.

There is no guarantee in any doctor.

There is no guarantee in any surgeon.

There is no guarantee in any nurse.

Jesus is our only guarantee to heal us from our heads down to our feet if it's in His will, but if it's not in His will He will still be glorified through our sickness that will sink into someone's heart to hold onto Jesus.

There is no guarantee for anyone to win all the time.

There is no guarantee for anyone to always get what they want.

There is no guarantee for you and me to always be right about what we say and do.

Jesus Christ, our Lord and Savior, is our only guarantee to give us His prize of eternal life because Jesus already won our race on that cross on Mount Calvery over a thousand years ago.

There is Nothing Wrong with Jesus

There is nothing wrong with Jesus who is nothing but the love of God forever and ever.

There is something wrong with me and you who were born in sin, which means there is something wrong with me and you.

There is nothing wrong with Jesus, who is perfect in all he says and does, but there is something wrong with me and you who can say something wrong and do something wrong and not even realize it until the Holy Spirit lets us know we were wrong.

There is nothing wrong with Jesus who holds me and you together and keeps us from falling apart over things we have no control over.

There is something wrong with me and you who can act like we own something and call it our own and then can want to throw it all away if things don't always go our way.

There is nothing wrong with Jesus who we can empty all of our hearts out to and we won't be misunderstood.

There is something wrong with me and you who can empty all of our hearts out to an enemy who we just don't know to be an enemy.

There is nothing wrong with Jesus who is the righteous King of kings and Lord of lords to be right about all that he says and does forever and ever.

There is something wrong with me and you who can believe that all of our works are right with the Lord who doesn't overlook even one wrong thing in our hearts not being like Him.

There is nothing wrong with Jesus who is the origin of wellness that he gives to me and you who can get sick and will want to not eat anything that is not good for us to eat while we are sick, but when we are well, we don't care to see the need to eat right like we should every day.

There is nothing wrong with Jesus who has no blame and no flaws and does not make mistakes, but there is something wrong with me and you and even an animal can sense that we are flawed in sin and be frightened of us.

There is nothing wrong with Jesus who goes out of His way to save the uttermost sinner from being lost in sin, but me and you can want to judge and look down on anyone who is struggling with being obedient to Jesus as if me and you have no sins and don't fall short of the glory of God.

True Love is in Actions

True love is in actions and not in words that can say I love you with ease, only for it to turn out that those words were full of hot air.

True love is in actions, which are real proof coming from the heart when words can have no real evidence to convince you and me to believe that true love needs no actions to back it up.

There is no true love without actions of love, no matter how many words of love are spoken from the tip of the tongue.

True love is seen in actions when words of love are like a bubble that can burst in thin air.

True love is in actions that are very bold and know no fear in the presence of anyone great or small who can feel the power of true love's actions to get their attention in one way or in another way.

True love is in actions that are far more true than words of love that can mean good and well while being caught up in the moment and can spiral down in a matter of minutes.

True love is in actions that will not spiral downhill when the going gets tough.

Actions of love will ride out the tough times for years and years and deal with the ups and downs of life.

True love is in actions that Jesus Christ proved to be true because his actions were seen on the cross that He hung on to save us from our sins that originated from the devil's hatred for God.

There is no love in our sins that Jesus became on the cross through His actions of love for all the world to be saved in Him who is God's true love that was sent from heaven to this dying, sinful world.

The Spiritual Career is Eternal

The spiritual career is eternal because only spiritual things are eternal in the Lord, who is not against anyone having a career to better their lives.

The spiritual career is not about getting rich and wealthy like careers in this world are about; those careers are temporary in our lives and will leave us going to our graves knowing nothing.

All the careers in this world are nothing good to enter into heaven where they will be of no good use to God who gives all of His children a spiritual career to spread the gospel of Jesus Christ to all the world.

The spiritual career is eternal for anyone to have for believing in Jesus Christ to be saved from our sins that hate our spiritual career that we can take with us to heaven when Jesus comes back again to give us eternal life beyond the careers of the world that will pass away one day.

It's no sin against God to have a career as long as we use it to build up the church, winning souls to be saved in Jesus Christ, whose career was to make fishers of men to be saved in Him.

The spiritual career is eternal, which all the angels in heaven and all the unfallen worlds truly know to be their purpose for existing so that they can love and obey God forever and ever.

Lucifer and the fallen angels didn't love their spiritual careers that God gave them; they wanted to create their own careers to be better than all that God had given to them because they thought it was not enough for them to enjoy the riches and wealth of God's spiritual eternal things in heaven.

Many people will have a good career in this world, but their career will go to their heads and cause them to believe they are so much better than those who don't have a career.

The weakest Christian in the church has a much better career that is spiritual to make this world a better place to live in by their Godly lifestyles than ungodly rich people using their careers for evil and making this world worse and worse to live in.

The spiritual career is eternal in Jesus Christ, who gave all of His children spiritual things in the church that He is the head of to reveal every self-ambition and career person not being like Him who originated careers for the good of building up His church.

For Granted

We can take our minds for granted if we think on whatever isn't like Jesus, who should be in our thoughts day after day.

We can take our eyes for granted if we only love to see anything that's not like Jesus, who we should love to keep our eyes on in His holy word where we can see Jesus.

The bible scriptures are always true about Jesus, but many church folks aren't always being like Jesus.

We can take our ears for granted if we only love to hear words not like Jesus, who we should love to hear about with our ears day after day.

We can take our mouths for granted if we only love to talk about anything not like Jesus, who we should love to talk about day after day, especially to unbelievers.

We can take our arms for granted if we only love to hug anyone who is like Jesus, who wants us to also hug our enemies who need a hug that can soften their hearts.

We can take our hands for granted if we only pick up and hold things not like Jesus, who wants us to pick up good things and hold good things in our hands to give to those who need it most.

We can take our legs for granted if we only love to stand up all the time to not be like Jesus, who wants us to bow down on our knees to pray to Him if we are physically able to do it.

We can take our feet for granted if we only love to walk and run to mischief and not be like Jesus who loves for us to walk and run the race of our faith in Him who has a heaven to take us to when He comes back again on the clouds of glory.

We can take our choices for granted if we only choose anything that's not like Jesus, who wants us to choose to love Him and keep His Commandments day after day.

We can take our hearts for granted if we hold onto ill feelings not being like Jesus, who wants us to forgive one another to be like Him who said to His heavenly Father, "Forgive them for they do not know what they do."

Jesus said that as He hung on the cross that He shed His blood on and died on in our place to save us from our sins and rose from the grave on the third day to give us His free gift of eternal life if we only believe in Him.

We can take our bodies for granted if we use our bodies to do our own will to reject the Holy Spirit from living in our bodies that are the temples where God's Holy Spirit dwells day after day.

The Holy Spirit lived in Jesus Christ when He lived in this sinful world and committed no sins against God for Jesus to be our high priest in heaven and make our pleas before God.

Doesn't Come Anywhere Close

The best thing in this world doesn't come anywhere close to the very least thing in heaven because we can't even imagine the eternal things that Jesus has for us in heaven.

The most beautiful thing in this world doesn't come anywhere close to the pleasant things in heaven because we don't know what beauty really is until we get to heaven where the pleasant things look so much more beautiful than the most beautiful things in this world.

The best technology in this world doesn't come anywhere close to the smallest simple things in heaven because we are so very far behind the smallest simple things in heaven that can baffle this world.

The greatest mind in this world doesn't come anywhere close to the least intelligent mind in heaven because we are mortal and don't know the meaning of the most simple word from heaven if the Holy Spirit doesn't reveal to us what it means.

The greatest treasure in this world doesn't come anywhere close to the cheapest things in heaven because the wealthiest people in this world are like trash in a dumpster compared to the cheapest things in heaven.

All the wealth in this world doesn't come anywhere close to anyone having the least stars on their crowns in heaven because just one star on a crown in heaven is eternal wealth worth so much more than all the money in this world.

The most successful person in this world doesn't come anywhere close to even the least ranking angel in heaven because that angel is eternal and will achieve much greater eternal success beyond the successes of mortal beings whose lives are like a shadow moving across the landscape and will disappear under God's bright, shining sunlight.

So Naked Before the Lord

We all are the same, so naked before the Lord every day that we live to put on some clothes to cover up our nakedness before one another.

We all are the same, so naked before the Lord who sees all of our thoughts being so naked to Him, whether our thoughts are good or evil.

We all are the same, so naked before the Lord who sees all of our motives and intentions being so naked to Him, whether our motives and intentions be good or evil.

We can cover up our nakedness before one another because we know that it's wrong for us to walk around with no clothes on our bodies; we can only do that in the privacy of our homes if we have no one else living with us from day to day.

Even our house pets can look at us so strangely if we are walking around in the house naked in front of them.

We are so naked in our sins before the Lord who will cloth our sins in His righteousness if we confess and repent and turn to Jesus, who makes us right before God.

We all are the same, so naked before the Lord who sees our spiritual nakedness that we can cover up in front of each other in the secretness of our hearts that the Lord sees to be so naked to Him every day that we live.

We can clothe our hearts with deception that is so naked before the Lord.

We can clothe our hearts with jealousy and envy that is so naked before the Lord.

We can clothe our hearts with covetousness that is so naked before the Lord.

We can clothe our hearts with lust that is so naked before the Lord.

We can clothe our hearts with discontentment that is so naked before the Lord.

We can clothe our hearts with selfishness that is so naked before the Lord.

We all were born into this world naked and many of us will leave this world with clothes on our bodies as we lay down in our caskets, but the destiny of all is so naked before the Lord even when many people believe that they are clothed in the Lord to give them eternal life.

We all are the same, so naked before the Lord Jesus Christ who gave up His life on the cross that was so naked for all the angels and the unfallen worlds to see so our souls would be spiritually clothed in the love of God who the devil can't ever undress.

Jesus proved this fact to all the world when He rose from the grave clothed in His eternal white robe.

As You and I Draw Closer and Closer to Jesus

As you and I draw closer and closer to Jesus, we should see that we need to confess and repent of more and more of our sins that Jesus will show to you and me as we draw closer and closer to Him.

As you and I draw closer and closer to Jesus, it should pain our hearts when we see that we pain Jesus for even sinning against Him in our ignorance because Jesus hates all sins whether it be knowing sins or ignorant sins.

As you and I draw closer and closer to Jesus, we should see that we can't take our Christian journey lightly or as a joke because Jesus doesn't take any lost soul lightly or as a joke and He judges everyone right and fair before a serious God in heaven.

As you and I draw closer and closer to Jesus, we should love one another more and more deeply because Jesus' love for us is deeper than the outer space that we will travel through on our way back to heaven if we are saved in Jesus Christ who we must believe in to be saved.

You and I can't draw closer and closer to Jesus if we believe that we can make excuses for our sins.

You and I can't draw closer and closer to Jesus if we take one another's soul salvation as a joke as if what we say and do before one another has no kind of effect to cause any one of us to draw closer to Jesus or to pull away from Jesus in some kind of way.

As you and I draw closer and closer to Jesus, we should very well hate more and more sin that can creep into the church so smooth and clever that we can take it lightly and overlook it.

As you and I draw closer and closer to Jesus, we should get cut up more and more of God's holy word to pain our hearts so that we confess our sins and repent.

As you and I draw closer and closer to Jesus, it will be impossible for us to not examine ourselves and shun every appearance of evil that the Holy Spirit will show to us outside the church and inside the church.

As you and I draw closer and closer to Jesus, we should have no desire to slack up on Jesus and give Him less and less of our worship, time, talent, tithes and obedience.

As you and I draw closer and closer to Jesus, it will be impossible to not go through any trials and temptations that we can also go through right in the church for Jesus' holy name sake.

As you and I draw closer and closer to Jesus, it will be impossible not to get a spiritual heart surgery that will be spiritually painful to us for Jesus to cut out our heart of stony sins that we can bring with us to church to rub off on one another who can think nothing of it and let it pollute the church.

As you and I draw closer and closer to Jesus, we should have no desire to want to be a friend to this sinful world but instead desire to win souls to Jesus by telling the truth in love, writing the truth in love, and most of all living the truth of Jesus in love to especially unbelievers.

Divorce Can Come From

Divorce can come from lack of getting affection or getting no affection.

Divorce can come from lack of communication or no communication.

Divorce can come from too many disagreements.

Divorce can come from not spending enough time together.

Divorce can come from being separated from each other.

Divorce can come from not trusting one another.

Divorce can come from lying to each other.

Divorce can come from abuse.

Divorce can come from trying to control one another.

Divorce can come from being unfaithful.

Divorce can come from getting into too much debt.

Divorce can come from changing for the worst on each other.

Divorce can come from not listening to one another.

Divorce can come from not providing for one another's needs.

Divorce can come from letting others come between you and your spouse.

Divorce can come from not being in the same faith.

Divorce can come from neglecting one another.

Divorce can come from being out of work.

Divorce can come from being lazy.

Divorce can come from working too much.

Divorce can come from falling out of love with each other.

Divorce can come from having no more attraction for each other.

Jesus Christ will never divorce His wife, the church, that can fall short and lack spiritual affection for Jesus.

Jesus Christ will never divorce His wife, the church, that can fall short and lack communication with Jesus.

Jesus Christ will never divorce His wife, the church, that can fall short and lack agreements with Jesus.

Jesus Christ will never divorce His wife, the church, that can fall short and lack peace with Jesus.

Jesus Christ will never divorce His wife, the church, that can fall short and not spend quality time with Jesus.

Jesus Christ will never divorce His wife, the church, that can fall short and fail to be with Jesus through good days and bad days.

Jesus Christ will never divorce His wife, the church, that can fall short and lack trust in Jesus.

Jesus Christ will never divorce His wife, the church, that can fall short and lack truthfulness to Jesus.

Jesus Christ will never divorce His wife, the church, that can fall short and not be good to Jesus.

Jesus Christ will never divorce His wife, the church, that can fall short and lack faithfulness to Jesus.

Jesus Christ will never divorce His wife, the church, that can fall short and not be a brother's keeper and be in spiritual debt to Jesus.

Jesus Christ will never divorce His wife, the church, that can fall short and change on Jesus for the worst, even if things are good in the church.

Jesus Christ will never divorce His wife, the church, that can fall short and fail to listen to the Holy Spirit, who Jesus sent to this world to teach the church all the truth about Him.

Jesus Christ will never divorce His wife, the church, that can fall short and fail to provide for souls' spiritual needs that Jesus equipped the church to do.

Jesus Christ will never divorce His wife, the church, that can fall short and fail to stand firm on her true doctrines which can compromise her belief in Jesus with the people of the world.

Jesus Christ will never divorce His wife, the church, that can fall short in being equally yoked which is the only way to be truly married to Jesus.

Jesus Christ will never divorce His wife, the church, that can fall short and be lacking in being with Jesus in His holy word and in prayer without ceasing which is neglecting Jesus.

Jesus Christ will never divorce His wife, the church, that can fall short and be lacking in work for Jesus to build up the church.

Jesus Christ will never divorce His wife, the church, that can fall short and be lacking in enthusiasm about uplifting Jesus' holy name even before spiritually lazy so-called Christians in the church.

Jesus Christ will never divorce His wife, the church, that can fall short and be lacking in not working enough for Jesus, while being able to do more work for Jesus.

Jesus Christ will never divorce His wife, the church, that can fall short and be lacking peace among church leaders and congregations that only Jesus can bring on one accord when things get out of order in the church.

Jesus Christ will never divorce His wife, the church, that can fall short and fail to spend good quality time with Jesus, who loves to spend time with His wife every second, minute and hour of each and every day of the week.

Spiritual divorce comes from straying away from Jesus to love worshipping idols that can be anyone or anything that we love more than Jesus, who we can divorce even in unseen ways.

The Christian Man
and the Man of the World

One day, the Christian man and the man of the world met up at the crossroads of life.

The Christian man was on the road to heaven and the man of the world was on the road to hell.

As soon as they met at the crossroads, the Christian man said to the man of the world, "I am no better than you, only different from you who God loves too."

The man of the world responded to the Christian man, asking, "How are you so different from me when you need to eat food, take a shower and work a job like me?"

The Christian man said, "That is so true. We are the same in doing the things we need to do to survive in this world."

The man of the world said to the Christian man, "We both need water to drink, clothes on our backs, shoes on our feet, a roof over our heads and we both need a bed to lay down in to get a good night's sleep. How can we be so different?"

The Christian man responded, "We are surely the same when it comes to the things that our flesh needs from day to day."

Just before the Christian man and the man of the world began to go their separate ways at the crossroads, the Christian man was filled with the Holy Spirit to be like Jesus.

The man of the world was filled with living in his sins to be like the devil and be so different from the Christian man.

So they departed from each other according to their choosing of who they would love and obey.

The Christian man chose to love Jesus and keep His Commandments, and the man of the world chose to love and obey the ways of this world.

The difference between the Christian man and the man of the world as they stood at the crossroads pointing toward heaven or hell is that the Christian man repented of his sins and turned to Jesus, but the man of the world held onto his sins to live for the devil.

If You and I Harden Our Hearts

If you and I harden our hearts against anyone who Jesus gave up His life on the cross and rose from the grave to save, then you and I harden our hearts against Jesus.

It's so easy to harden our hearts against anyone we don't like, but anyone who opens up and empties all of their hearts in confession and repentance unto Jesus will be accepted by Jesus who has an eternal soft heart for every sinner who He wants to save from their sins.

Even some church folks will harden their hearts against you and me, but they are no match for Jesus who we hurt in many seen and unseen ways.

Even when we do this, Jesus will forgive us with loving, open arms as if we never hurt His heart.

If you and I harden our hearts against anyone outside the church and inside the church, then we harden our hearts against Jesus Christ who all souls belong to.

Only Jesus is worthy to harden His heart against anyone who rejects him after having the opportunity to repent and turn to Him.

If you and I harden our hearts against anyone, then we also harden our hearts against ourselves because we choose to hold onto our sinful nature that has nothing good about it and will not set us free from even not forgiving ourselves for hardening our hearts against ourselves.

If there is anyone in heaven and on earth who has the right to harden his heart against anyone, it is truly the Lord Jesus Christ who took on all of the world's hard sins to make the cross so hard and cruel for Jesus to shed His blood on to save us all from our very hard sins.

Jesus didn't harden his heart against us and became sin on the cross for us.

Only Jesus deserves to harden His heart against all who were born in sin, which includes you and me who would have no possible way to be like Jesus if we harden our hearts against anyone who Jesus owns to take with Him to heaven or cast into hell.

If you and I harden our hearts against anyone, then we also harden our hearts against Jesus who knows everyone's hearts to judge every motive and intention to be right or wrong and good or evil beyond any actions.

An action can look evil in anyone's eyes who cannot see a good reason from the heart of someone; even killing someone else in self-defense.

Self-defense is a good thing to protect your life, but someone else can see it as an evil action.

The Lord will not harden His heart against anyone who kills someone else in self-defense.

We live in a sinful world where many people harden their hearts against innocent victims protecting themselves from hardcore criminals who have hardened their hearts against good, law-abiding citizens to do us the evils of harm and danger and death.

If you and I harden our hearts against anyone, even our enemies outside the church and inside the church, then we are no better than a murderer because we can spiritually kill someone by holding grudges and hating someone who the Lord can get vengeance on to save their soul.

If you and I harden our hearts against anyone, then we harden our hearts against our own souls which will be lost when that someone we hardened our hearts against may very well be saved in the Lord for repenting of their sins and turning to Him before it's too late.

We don't own anything in this world to harden our hearts against anyone, even if they kill our loved ones who are most precious to us.

We don't own that, but God owns it to give and take away for His reasons that are too high up for anyone to understand.

If you and I harden our hearts against anyone who Jesus laid down His life for on the cross, then we crucify Jesus over again to make His death so worthless for anyone to choose to repent and die to self to live for Jesus, no matter what bad things they've done to you and me.

No one's sins are too hard for Jesus to forgive.

Jesus didn't harden His heart against us who were born in the hardened heart of sinning against the Lord even in our ignorance.

Jesus Christ, the Lord, didn't harden His heart against those Pharisees and religious leaders who had Him crucified.

Jesus didn't harden His heart against Judas who betrayed him.

Jesus didn't harden His heart against Peter who denied him three times.

Jesus didn't harden His heart against those Roman soldiers who hit Him in the face, spit in His face, beat him and nailed Him on the cross.

Jesus said to His heavenly Father, God, "Forgive them for they do not know what they do."

Who are you and I not to forgive others who do us evil, for we are not worthy to harden our hearts against anyone who we are not better than to be in favor with God.

God didn't harden His heart against King David for sleeping with another man's wife and setting him up to be killed in the heat of battle in a war.

God forgave King David because he repented of his sins with all of his heart unto God.

If you and I harden our hearts against anyone who hates us and even lies on us in the church, then we harden our hearts against what the Lord can do for us to chastise our enemies on His time that can soften our enemies' hearts to make peace with you and me without even really knowing that it's the Lord who is working on their hardened hearts.

If you and I harden our hearts against anyone, then we harden our hearts against the Lord as well as against ourselves.

It will truly be seen on judgment day that the wicked can't blame anyone but themselves and God will cast them into fire and brimstone.

You and I can harden our hearts against ourselves and not even see it.

We can take it out on the Lord for allowing us to choose whatever we want to do until it catches up with us and we realize we are so frail and regret the mess we made in our lives because we were so hard on ourselves.

If you and I harden our hearts against the Lord, then we will harden our hearts against ourselves and anyone else while we pretend like we are so happy-go-lucky in our outward appearance.

There is nothing that the Lord can't do to soften anyone's heart, even if it happens on judgment day that all the wicked will bow down to God.

The wicked will know too late that a hardened heart can't win against God to even soften it to acknowledge that God is God while being cast into hell's fire and brimstone.

God doesn't want to be out of His character and destroy what He created in love for His pleasure for all existence, but by this point it's too late for the wicked to turn back to God, whose purpose for everyone's hearts is to love Him.

Without Your Approval, My Lord

My mother and father could not have procreated and produced me without Your approval, My Lord and Savior Jesus Christ who created human beings to procreate and produce more human beings.

O, my Lord God, You created the very first human beings on earth and allowed them to procreate with other human beings to populate this world with billions of human beings today.

My Lord, you created all creatures to procreate and make other creatures in this world.

O, my Lord, You even created the birds and reptiles and insects and allowed them to procreate.

From the beginning of this world, nothing in this world could procreate without Your approval, O Lord, the creator of procreation.

O Lord, You didn't create the angels to procreate and make other angels.

We human beings are so blessed that you didn't create the angels to procreate.

If You, O Lord, had created the angels to procreate then the fallen angels from heaven would have been able to procreate and make countless other evil angels to tempt human beings to sin against You, O Lord.

It would surely be too much temptation for every human being to bear from day to day.

O Lord, You are perfect in everything that you do and never make any mistakes because you foreknew before You created the angels that it would be so wrong to create angels that could procreate.

We human beings on earth have a very hard time with the devil and his fallen angels, so just imagine if they could procreate — there would be billions of more evil angels to tempt the human race to sin against God, who foreknew that the fallen angels would do just that.

Many human beings will have children and raise them to have nothing to do with the Creator God who allowed them to be born into this world to worship Him in spirit and truth, which is every human being's true purpose in this world.

If human beings can procreate other human beings who choose to rebel against God, then it would be much worse if God had created the angels to procreate and produce other angels when especially the devil and his fallen angels would procreate countless numbers of nothing but evil angels to try to possess every human being as well as all of the animals and reptiles and birds and make them turn against all the human beings living on earth.

O my Lord God and Savior Jesus Christ, You predestined all things to not go beyond Your approval that all existence can't disapprove of and change Your origin of creation of all things in heaven and on earth and in the unfallen worlds.

Like We've Never Been Through

We can go through something hard and it may seem to last forever and feel like we'll never make it through our hardship.

We can feel pain in our bodies and it can seem like the pain will never go away because we may feel some pain that can last for years and years.

We can get used to feeling pain like it's air to breathe out of our nostrils so we can live from day to day.

We can also live with pain, whether it's emotional or physical pain.

Every disappointment and bad experience we have in our lives will be like we've never been through it when Jesus Christ comes back again on the clouds of glory to take us with Him back to heaven if we are saved in Him.

All of the pain we felt and still feel today will be like we've never felt any pain or heartache and will be like it never existed in our lives when Jesus gives us our new immortal bodies so we can be perfect forever and ever with no trace of sin that is the origin of everyone's pain.

All of the trials and temptations that we've been through and are going through today will go for as long as we live, but if we live for Jesus' holy name sake it will surely be like we've never been through any of it when we die being saved in Jesus.

When Jesus comes back again on the clouds of glory, He will raise us up out of the grave in our glorious bodies and we will be heaven-bound for eternal life.

If we are alive when Jesus comes back again, He will change us from mortal to immortality in the twinkling of an eye and all of our pain and suffering will be like we've never had it because it will flee from us faster than the speed of light that is like a slow turtle moving on the ground compared to Jesus.

We real, true Christians especially will go through even unexpected hardships that can come upon us at any time of the day to test our faith in Jesus, and it can be painful.

One day, it all will be like we've never been through any bad things in this sinful world when Jesus Christ, our Lord, comes back again on the clouds of glory with all of His angels.

All the trials we went through will be like a bad dream and flash by us so fast like a light in the night to surely pass away.

O what a glorious bright day it will be when Jesus Christ comes back again to take us to heaven like we've never been through any hardships.

Jesus will bring to our memories the hardships that he's been through to save us from our sins and we will see the nail prints in His hands and feet to be evidence of the pain and suffering that He went through for us.

Jesus will wipe away our tears that originate from pain that we do experience in this sinful world, but Jesus will give us eternal life like we've never been through anything bad in this sinful world that will one day pass away like it was never here with sin in it.

We Church Folks

We church folks can't be like Jesus and be like the people of the world at the same time.

It's either one or the other who we will be like from day to day.

We church folks can't please Jesus and please the people of the world at the same time.

It's either one or the other who we will please from day to day.

We church folks can't bring Jesus to the church with us and bring the world with us to church at the same time.

It's either one or the other being in the church with us.

We church folks can't worship Jesus Christ and worship this world at the same time.

It's either one or the other to be worshipped from day to day.

We church folks can't be a slave to Jesus and a slave to this world at the same time.

It's either one or the other to be our master from day to day.

We church folks can't love Jesus and love this world at the same time.

It's either one or the other for us to love from day to day.

We church folks can't be a friend to Jesus and be a friend to this sinful world at the same time.

It's either one or the other for us to be a friend to from day to day.

We church folks can't believe in Jesus Christ and believe in this sinful world at the same time.

It's either one or the other for us to believe in from day to day.

We church folks can't lay up our treasures in heaven and lay up our treasures in this world at the same time.

It's either one or the other for us to lay up our treasures in from day to day.

We church folks can't live for Jesus and live for the prince of this world at the same time.

It's either one or the other who we will live for from day to day.

We church folks can't dress in modest apparel and dress like the people of the world at the same time.

It's either one or the other for us to dress like from day to day.

We church folks can't be a Christian and be like the people of the world at the same time.

It's either one or the other for us to be from day to day.

We church folks can't be converted and be like the people of the world at the same time.

It's either one or the other for us to be from day to day.

We church folks can't be convicted of our sins and live like the people of the world at the same time.

It's either one or the other for us to be from day to day.

We church folks can't live a renewed life in Jesus Christ and live in our sins at the same time.

It's either one or the other for us to live in from day to day.

We church folks can't keep our eyes on Jesus and keep our eyes on this sinful world at the same time.

It's either one or the other for us to keep our eyes on from day to day.

We church folks can't put our hope in Jesus and put our hope in this sinful world at the same time.

It's either one or the other for us to put our hope in from day to day.

We church folks can't have the Holy Spirit in us and have the devil in us at the same time.

It's either one or the other who will be in us.

We church folks can't be saved in Jesus Christ and live for the devil at the same time.

It's either one or the other who we will chose to be the master of our lives.

We church folks can't pray without ceasing and live like we are self-made at the same time.

It's either one or the other to stand firm on surely being Jesus and not ourselves who have no power to answer anyone's prayers from day to day.

We church folks can't live a Christian life and a double life at the same time.

It's either one or the other for us to reap what we sow.

We church folks can't be a witness of Jesus and be out of control of ourselves at the same time.

It's either one or the other for people to see who we really are about from day to day.

We church folks can't be Jesus' disciples and not love one another at the same time.

It's either one or the other that the people of the world will surely see, especially while being a visitor in our church.

We church folks can't be a new creature in Jesus Christ and not give Jesus our all at the same time day after day.

It's either one or the other that will surely tell on us inside the church and outside the church.

We church folks can't be selfless like Jesus and be full of ourselves at the same time.

It's either one or the other for us to give what we can give to others or be stingy and hold onto things that we don't' need that someone else needs that will be a blessing to them.

We church folks can't be a good example to even babes in Jesus and compromise our faith and works in Jesus with those who know the truth about the bible and don't live the truth in the bible.

It's either one or the other that will cause us to have a good effect or a bad effect on even babes in Jesus.

We church folks can only be saved in Jesus Christ one day at a time, because that's what it takes to be like Jesus no matter how strong and mature we are in the Lord.

We all will fall short of His glory, even in a bad thought that causes us to not be like Jesus.

Jesus will save us from our sins for believing in Him one day at a time.

We church folks can choose to love and obey Jesus regardless of the people of the world rejecting Jesus by their free will choices from day to day.

If You Put Your Trust In

If you put your trust in money, it will cause you to want more and more of it.

If you put your trust in material things, it will cause you to want more and more of them.

If you put your trust in people, they will cause you to be more and more disappointed.

If you put your trust in yourself, that will cause you to be more and more proud of yourself.

If you put your trust in life, it will cause you to be more and more afraid to die.

If you put your trust in this world, it will cause you to lay up more and more of your treasures in this world.

If you put your trust in Jesus Christ, you will be more and more content.

If you put your trust in Jesus Christ, you will be more and more joyful.

If you put your trust in Jesus Christ, you will be more and more blessed.

If you put your trust in Jesus Christ, you will be more and more humble.

If you put your trust in Jesus Christ, you will be more and more loving.

If you put your trust in Jesus Christ, you will be more and more bold to live for Jesus before your enemies who can't take your life if Jesus doesn't allow them to.

If you put your trust in Jesus Christ, you will be more and more like Jesus and not be a friend to this sinful world that is not a friend to you and me for believing in Jesus Christ.

A Stranger

You and I can sometimes have a better conversation with a stranger than with someone we know.

You and I can sometimes get a good laugh with a stranger when we can't get a laugh at all with someone we know.

You and I can sometimes feel closer to a stranger than with someone we know.

You and I can sometimes read the mind of a stranger better than reading the mind of someone we know.

You and I can sometimes feel like we know a stranger more than someone we have known for a long time.

You and I can sometimes love a stranger more than someone we know.

You and I can sometimes get more love from a stranger than from someone we know.

You and I can sometimes get more respect from a stranger than we get from someone we know.

You and I can sometimes get more help from a stranger than from someone we know.

You and I can sometimes get more encouragement from a stranger than from someone we know.

You and I can sometimes have more peace with a stranger than with someone we know.

You and I can sometimes talk about our Lord and Savior Jesus Christ with a stranger more than we can with someone we know.

You and I can sometimes cheer up a stranger better than we can cheer up someone we know.

You and I can sometimes be forgiven by a stranger and not be forgiven by someone we know.

You and I can sometimes believe that a stranger is telling us the truth and not believe someone we know.

You and I can sometimes learn something good from a stranger and learn nothing good from someone we know.

You and I can sometimes trust a stranger more than someone we know.

You and I can sometimes understand a stranger better than someone we know.

You and I can sometimes be more of a blessing to a stranger than to someone we know.

You and I can sometimes use our spiritual gifts from the Lord to uplift and encourage some strangers to keep their eyes on Jesus better than some of those in the church who we know.

You and I can sometimes be more blessed from the Lord by a stranger than by someone who we know in the church.

You and I can sometimes get some better Godly wise advice from a stranger than we can get from some of those we know in the church.

There are some strangers who can be unaware angels and you and I would not know it but will feel a strong presence of the Lord from them.

You and I can be in church and sometimes feel the presence of the devil from some of those who we know are not like Jesus Christ, who you and I can also not be like even to a stranger if we are selfish in our ways.

You and I can sometimes see evil in the eyes of a stranger, that lets us know we need to be very cautious around them, but if we see evil in the eyes of someone we know in the church, we need to be even more cautious as we wonder if he or she still has the Holy Spirit dwelling in them.

I Live in a World

I live in a world where many people love to give human beings the glory and praise that only Jesus is worthy of day after day.

It's the Lord Jesus Christ who keeps the breath in the body of all the living human beings as well as the animals, reptiles, insects, birds and all the fish in the oceans, seas, lakes, rivers, ponds, streams and bays.

It's Jesus who created all things and not human beings who are not worthy to get the glory and praise that belongs to Jesus Christ forever and ever.

I live in a world where many people will worship human beings like they're God to bow down unto day after day, but only Jesus is worthy to worship and bow down unto in our prayers unto Him and not unto any human being who will fail us in some kind of way.

I live in a world where many people will live their lives unto human beings who were born in sin to one day die under the sun, when Jesus is beyond the sun and will live forever and ever and have an eternal heaven to take us to when He comes back again on the clouds of glory.

I live in a world where many church folks will put human beings up on a pedestal as if they are worthy to be the head of the church over Jesus Christ who is worthy to be the head of the church that is all about Jesus who gave up His life on the cross for us.

I live in a world where many people will give up their lives to save the life of human beings, but will not give up their lives for Jesus' holy name sake.

Only Jesus can give anyone who is saved in Him an afterlife to be eternal beyond mortal human beings who can't raise the dead.

I live in a sinful world where so many people will keep their eyes on human beings who are not perfect to have sins breaking God's holy law.

Only Jesus Christ had no sins when He lived in this sinful world where every human being would be wise to keep their eyes on Jesus who is perfect in all of His ways.

Jesus is the way, the truth and the life for us to live doing God's holy will.

Heavyweight

Many people need to hear some heavyweight sermons about the Lord Jesus Christ who was no lightweight opponent against the devil, especially in the wilderness for forty days and forty nights when Jesus knocked out the devil with the word of God.

We can easily fall asleep spiritually during the lightweight sermons in the church that can bore people and make them fall asleep during church.

We are living in a heavyweight, sinful world that will waste no time knocking anyone out with the devil's sinful, heavyweight bout of lies and deceptions that have knocked out many people, even in the church.

Many people will take God's holy word lightly because it seems lightweight to them.

They see no change in their lives that moves them to confess and repent of their sins that they cherish and think are a normal thing day after day.

The sins they take as lightweight are surely heavyweight in the eyes of God who hates all sin but loves every sinner to be saved in His Son, Jesus Christ.

Time is running out in this world and every Christian who is mature in God's word should be a heavyweight Christian to knock the devil and his human agents out with the truth of God's holy word that should be seen in every Christian's life before unbelievers.

Our Christian lives should be so heavyweight that when we are in the presence of unbelievers they should feel and see the heavyweight difference in us and see that we are truly about Jesus Christ, even in the way that we dress in modest apparel.

The devil knows that we Christians worship a heavyweight God and we Christians must live like we are not lightweights in our trials that can change an unbeliever's life to live for Jesus because of our heavyweight faith in Jesus.

With Their Words

Many people are very clever with their words that cause evil doings to be so smooth going and look so innocent, especially to many feeble-minded people.

Many people are very deceitful with their words that cause evil doings to look so right to do, especially in the eyes of many people who want change to benefit them.

Many people are very tactful in a bad way with their words and cause evil doings to look like they're a good thing to do in the presence of many out of control people who see no wrongs in doing whatever they want to do.

Many people are very good with their words and cause evil doings to look so trustworthy, especially to many people who despise good people who they don't trust to have good motives and intentions.

Many church folks are very mean with their words, especially when they're spoken to those who they believe to be better than to cause evil doings of showing favoritism in the church.

Many church folks are very truthful with their words about Jesus bringing them from a mighty long way in their testimonies, but there are church folks who will use our testimonies for evil with their words and say that we need to move on beyond the past.

Many church folks are very spiritual with their words and they love to pray and talk about Jesus Christ, who we all need to love and obey.

There are church folks who love to say with their words, "I am only human," as an excuse for evil doings in the eyes of unbelievers which makes Jesus look so powerless to change their lives and make them a new creature in Him.

There are People Who Will

There are people who will try to talk you and me into to doing something that we don't want to do.

There are people who will try to talk you and me into doing something that we know is wrong to do.

There are people who just don't care to try to get you and me to go along with them in their selfish wrong-doings.

There are people who will try to drag you and me down in their evilness.

There are people who will try to control you and me to get us to go along with whatever they say.

There are people who will try to control you and me and try to get us to go along with whatever they do.

There are people who will try to make you and me look bad if we don't kiss up to them.

There are people who will talk bad about you and me if we move up beyond them in life.

There are people who will have nothing to do with you and me if we step on their toes with the truth of God's holy word that they are not living by.

There are people right in the church who will get envious of you and me if our spiritual gifts outshine their spiritual gifts.

There are people right in the church who will believe they are better than you and me if we are not on their educational level.

There are people right in the church who will judge you and me to have sinned against God if we are going through some bad things that seem to have no end.

There are people right in the church who will love you and me like Jesus no matter how slow we are in growing spiritually in the Lord.

There are people right in the church who will love you and me like Jesus, regardless of whether we stumble or fall into sinning against God.

There are people right in the church who will love you and me like Jesus, even if we are changeable in our ways while they are stable in their ways to be a living example to us to see Jesus being always the same way in them.

There are people right in the church who will love you and me like Jesus, even if they don't see Jesus in you and me.

They will pray for you and me to confess and repent of our sins and turn to Jesus who we can stray away from right in the church for Jesus to say, "Depart from Me, I never knew you."

Trauma Can Shatter

Trauma can shatter anyone's esteem.

Trauma can shatter anyone's identity.

Trauma can shatter anyone's dreams.

Trauma can shatter anyone's emotions.

Trauma can shatter anyone's mind.

Trauma can shatter anyone's innocence.

Trauma can shatter anyone's outlook on life.

Trauma can shatter anyone's life.

Trauma can shatter anyone's achievements.

Trauma can shatter anyone's confidence.

Trauma can shatter anyone's pride.

Trauma can shatter anyone's heart.

Trauma can shatter anyone's love.

Trauma can shatter anyone's hopes.

Trauma can shatter anyone's faith.

Trauma can shatter anyone's determination.

Trauma can shatter anyone's courage.

Trauma can shatter any child's esteem.

Trauma can shatter any child's growth.

Trauma can shatter any child's innocence.

Trauma can shatter any child's life.

There is no trauma too hard for Jesus to not use for our good of giving a testimony about Jesus bringing us through our trauma.

There is no trauma that Jesus can't heal us from for us to encourage others to put their trust in Jesus to get them through their trauma.

We are not too shattered by any trauma for Jesus not to put our lives back together.

All that we have to do is believe in Jesus Christ for us to claim, "I can do all things through Christ who strengthens me."

When Jesus Comes Back Again

When Jesus comes back again, it will be joyful to all the holy saints.

When Jesus comes back again, it will be miraculous to all the holy saints.

When Jesus comes back again, it will be wonderful to all the holy saints.

When Jesus comes back again, it will be rewarding to all the holy saints.

When Jesus comes back again, it will be extraordinary to all the holy saints.

When Jesus comes back again, it will be powerful to all the holy saints.

When Jesus comes back again, it will be great to all the holy saints.

When Jesus comes back again, it will be captivating to all the holy saints.

When Jesus comes back again, it will be real to all the holy saints.

When Jesus comes back again, it will be magnificent to all the holy saints.

When Jesus comes back again, it will be victorious to all the holy saints.

When Jesus comes back again, it will be unforgettable to all the holy saints.

When Jesus comes back again, it will be worth waiting for to all the holy saints.

When Jesus comes back again, it will be true to all the holy saints.

When Jesus comes back again, it will be brilliant to all the holy saints.

When Jesus comes back again, it will be trustworthy to all the holy saints.

When Jesus comes back again, it will be glorious to all the holy saints.

When Jesus comes back again, it will be beautiful to all the holy saints.

When Jesus comes back again, it will be well to all the holy saints.

When Jesus comes back again, it will be right to all the holy saints.

When Jesus comes back again, it will be holy to all the holy saints.

When Jesus comes back again, it will be an honor to all the holy saints.

When Jesus comes back again, it will be freedom to all the holy saints.

When Jesus comes back again, it will be out of this world to all the holy saints.

When Jesus comes back again, it will be visible to all the holy saints.

When Jesus comes back again, it will be justice to all the holy saints.

When Jesus comes back again, it will be peace to all the holy saints.

When Jesus comes back again, it will be God's love to all the holy saints.

When Jesus comes back again, it will be God's gift to all the holy saints.

When Jesus comes back again, it will be God's will to all the holy saints.

When Jesus comes back again, it will be admiration to all the holy saints.

When Jesus comes back again, it will be a big relief to all the holy saints.

When Jesus comes back again, it will be audible to all the holy saints.

When Jesus comes back again, it will be fulfilling to all the holy saints.

When Jesus comes back again, it will be amazing to all the holy saints.

When Jesus comes back again, it will be healing to all the holy saints.

When Jesus comes back again, it will be perfection to all the holy saints.

When Jesus comes back again, it will be healthy to all the holy saints.

When Jesus comes back again, it will be on time to all the holy saints.

When Jesus comes back again, it will be encouraging to all the holy saints.

When Jesus comes back again, it will be correct to all the holy saints.

When Jesus comes back again, it will be energizing to all the holy saints.

When Jesus comes back again, it will be successful to all the holy saints.

When Jesus comes back again, it will be good to all the holy saints.

When Jesus comes back again, it will be connection to all the holy saints.

When Jesus comes back again, it will be a blessing to all the holy saints.

When Jesus comes back again, it will be immortal to all the holy saints.

When Jesus comes back again, it will be communicating to all the holy saints.

When Jesus comes back again, it will be spiritual to all the holy saints.

When Jesus comes back again, it will be worthwhile to all the holy saints.

When Jesus comes back again, it will be complete to all the holy saints.

When Jesus comes back again, it will be warmth to all the holy saints.

When Jesus comes back again, it will be fearless to all the holy saints.

When Jesus comes back again, it will be breathtaking to all the holy saints.

When Jesus comes back again, it will be gazing to all the holy saints.

When Jesus comes back again, it will be divine to all the holy saints.

When Jesus comes back again, it will be wealth to all the holy saints.

When Jesus comes back again, it will be deliverance to all the holy saints.

When Jesus comes back again, it will be cheerful to all the holy saints.

When Jesus comes back again, it will be heaven to all the holy saints.

When Jesus comes back again, it will be the afterlife to all the holy saints.

When Jesus comes back again, it will be unity to all the holy saints.

When Jesus comes back again, it will be all tears wiped away to all the holy saints.

When Jesus comes back again, it will be all things made new to all the holy saints.

When Jesus comes back again, it will be all the holy saints living with Jesus Christ forever and ever.

When Jesus Christ comes back again it will be all the holy saints traveling through the outer space with Jesus and all the holy angels on the way back to heaven for all the unfallen worlds to see and be blessed.

When Jesus Christ, our Lord, comes back again it will be eternal life given to you and me for being saved in Jesus Christ, and we will join all the holy saints going with Jesus back to paradise that will last forever.

God Will Take You and Me to His Court

God will take you and me to His court in heaven where God will judge you and me who God accuses of sinning against Him.

Only God has every right to accuse you and me for sinning against Him, even in unseen ways along with seen ways, and we will see how wrong we are for sinning against God.

God will take you and me to His court in heaven where Jesus Christ is our lawyer to defend you and me so we will be found innocent before a holy and righteous God.

We must do our part to confess and repent of our sins and turn to Jesus to represent our case before God in heaven.

Only Jesus can prove you and me to be innocent before God through His righteousness that makes us perfect in God's eyesight when our righteousness is like filthy rags before God who you and I can't ever face up to without Jesus.

God sees you and me to be guilty of our sins before Him.

Only Jesus Christ, our Lord, can stand before God and plea our case, and that is what Jesus will do if we do our part and repent and turn to Him so He can wash us clean from our sins and God can kick the devil out of His court for making false accusations against you and me who are new creatures in Jesus Christ.

Jesus will plea everyone's case who loves Him and keeps His Commandments.

God will find all who believe in His Son, Jesus Christ, innocent before Him in His court in heaven.

God's court is open right now for sinners to get their heart right with Jesus before it's too late.

No one can represent themselves before God in His court in heaven because no one is worthy to say one word to God.

Only Jesus is worthy before God through the price He paid to save us from our sins.

Only Jesus could pay our price to give us His reward of eternal life that we are not worthy to receive.

Many people go to the courts in this world where a criminal can be found innocent and also an innocent person can receive millions of dollars for pain and suffering caused by a reckless person.

You and I and everyone else in this world are reckless before God in our sins that caused Jesus to suffer in pain on the cross.

Jesus died on the cross and rose from the grave to save us from our sins and give us undeserved wealth of eternal life when He comes back again on the clouds of glory.

You and I and everyone else must do our parts to confess and repent and live for Jesus before God who will find favor upon us and dismiss our cases in His heavenly court because of Jesus redeeming us back to Him with our robes washed in Jesus' blood.

Don't be Deceived

The Lord can't give spiritual things to anyone who is living in darkness.

Don't be deceived, the Holy Spirit can't dwell in anyone who is a liar, murderer, thief, fornicator, adulterer, abuser, gossiper, homosexual or boaster.

God is light and sin is darkness that breaks God's holy law that is light to us from God.

The Lord can't give spiritual things to anyone who has a form of Godliness but denies the power of the Holy Spirit that doesn't dwell in anyone who makes a practice of doing evil things day after day.

The Lord can't give spiritual things to anyone in the church if their lives are not in line with God's holy word, because the real, true church is the heart that loves and obeys the Lord beyond the outward appearance of assembling ourselves together in the church building.

Don't be deceived, the Lord can't give spiritual things to an unbeliever who can be in church for the wrong reasons, and sooner or later the Lord will shake him or her out of the church.

Don't be deceived, the Lord can't give spiritual things to a fool no matter how educated he or she may be, because spiritual things can only be given to anyone who has been born again to be a new creature in Jesus Christ.

Everyone who is in church hasn't been born again in the Holy Spirit because they're holding onto some unconfessed and unrepented sins.

Don't be deceived, because anyone who is living in their sins and truly knows that they are living in their sins doesn't have the light of Jesus in them no matter how holy and righteous they seem to appear.

The devil can appear to be an angel of light, but he is filled with total darkness every day.

The Lord can't give spiritual things to anyone who has the wrong motives for working for Him.

Don't be deceived, the Lord can't give His Holy Spirit to you and me if we are living in secret sins as if the Lord will excuse us of them because we appear outwardly to be holy.

The Lord can't give His spiritual things to anyone whose mind is in thoughts of unrighteousness day after day.

Spiritual-mindedness and carnal-mindedness cannot be in agreement unto the Lord, and a true child of God won't disagree.

It's Easy to Believe

It's easy to believe that we won't disobey the voice of the angel of the Lord.

Lot's wife disobeyed the angel of the Lord and looked back on Sodom and Gormorrah and turned into a pillar of salt.

Who are we to believe we won't look back on our possessions just before the closing probation on this world?

It's easy to believe that we won't be afraid of all the truth that may cost us our lives.

Abraham was afraid to tell all the truth that Sarah was his wife to keep the Egyptian soldiers from killing him, even though God could have protected him if Abraham had told the Egyptian soldiers that Sarah was his wife even though she was his sister.

It's easy to believe that we would not have disobeyed God like Moses disobeyed God and hit the rock that water came out of.

There are spiritual rocks that we can hit when the Lord tells us to speak to those spiritual rocks for His living waters to quench our thirsty souls in this wilderness world of sin being only like a dried-up water well.

It's easy to believe that we would not disobey God like Jonah disobeyed God to not go to Nineveh and tell the wicked people to repent.

Jonah wanted God to destroy the wicked people in Nineveh because they had caused his people to suffer greatly.

You and I can want God to punish those who cause great harm and even death upon our loved ones, which makes us no better than Jonah.

It's easy to believe that we would not lie to the Holy Spirit who Ananias and Sapphira lied to and fell dead.

If we know the truth of God's holy word and don't live it, we are liars to the Holy Spirit and die spiritually right in the church.

Even though we are alive physically and moving around, we will die spiritually for knowing what is right and not doing it.

It's easy to believe that we would not betray Jesus like Judas betrayed Him for thirty pieces of silver.

We can betray Jesus by being proud of ourselves for making achievements that Jesus allowed us to make.

We can betray Jesus with a kiss on His holy name that we can speak out openly to one another, while maybe making His holy name to be so worthless down in our hearts that may be filled with greed like Judas had in his heart.

It's easy to believe that we would not deny Jesus like Peter denied Him for the cock to crow three times.

We can deny Jesus even in little ways before even one another as well as in a big way and think nothing of it.

We are living in the last days and heading towards who we will truly worship being Jesus Christ or the prince of this world.

It's very possible that we may very well be alive when God closes His probation on this world for Jesus to stand up and say that it is finished.

If we are denying Jesus in any way today and know that we are doing it, then we will give into the fear of being killed for Jesus' holy name sake to receive the mark of the beast.

Now is the time for us to repent like Peter did after he denied Jesus three times.

Denying Jesus can be happening right in the church where we can want the glory and praise that only Jesus is worthy of that the holy angels know not to ever deny.

Everybody Can Choose
to Believe in Jesus Christ

Everybody will not think all of the same thoughts.

Everybody will not say all of the same words.

Everybody will not do all of the same things.

Everybody can choose to believe in Jesus Christ.

Everybody will not have all of the same ideas.

Everybody will not have all of the same talents.

Everybody will not have all of the same skills.

Everybody can choose to believe in Jesus Christ.

Everybody will not have all of the same understanding.

Everybody will not have all of the same knowledge.

Everybody will not have all of the same intelligence.

Everybody can choose to believe in Jesus Christ.

Everybody will not have all of the same appetite.

Everybody will not have all of the same tastebuds.

Everybody will not have all of the same motives.

Everybody can choose to believe in Jesus Christ.

Everybody will not have all of the same intentions.

Everybody will not have all of the same wants.

Everybody will not have all of the same needs.

Everybody can choose to believe in Jesus Christ.

Everybody will not have all of the same temptations.

Everybody will not have all of the same weaknesses.

Everybody will not have all of the same experiences.

Everybody can choose to believe in Jesus Christ.

Everybody will not have all of the same testimonies.

Everybody will not see eye to eye on everything.

Everybody will not hear all of the same things in the same way.

Everybody can choose to believe in Jesus Christ.

Everybody will not walk the same way.

Everybody will not run the same way.

Everybody will not talk the same way.

Everybody can choose to believe in Jesus Christ.

Everybody will not have all of the same desires.

Everybody will not have all of the same ambitions.

Everybody will not have all of the same courage.

Everybody can choose to believe in Jesus Christ.

Everybody will not make all of the same mistakes.

Everybody will not have all of the same flaws.

Everybody will not have all of the same habits.

Everybody can choose to believe in Jesus Christ.

Everybody will not ask all the same questions.

Everybody will not give all the same answers.

Everybody will not have all the same reasons.

Everybody can choose to believe in Jesus Christ.

Everybody will not have all the same feelings.

Everybody will not make all the same decisions.

Everybody will not have all the same ways.

Everybody can choose to believe in Jesus Christ to be saved all the same and receive eternal life all the same.

Those Kinds of People

There are those kinds of people who are too proud to accept something good that you and I offer to them.

There are those kinds of people who will block you and me on purpose to keep us from passing by them on the road.

There are those kinds of people who will believe that you and I are wrong for telling them the truth.

There are those kinds of people who will lie on you and me and feel good about it.

There are those kinds of people who just can't take no for an answer from you and me.

There are those kinds of people who see no wrong in themselves, but will surely see you and me being wrong for speaking our minds to them.

There are those kinds of church folks who are mean to you and me and are kind to those who are very well-educated like them.

There are those kinds of church folks who are envious of you and me and will cherish those who are not a threat to them in the church.

There are those kinds of church folks who will point their fingers at your sins and my sins and don't' see themselves having a bad, sinful effect on you and me in the church.

Let's you and me not be those kinds of church folks who will purposely try to make someone look bad because they aren't so well-put together in the church.

Let's you and me not be those kinds of church folks who believe they're too perfect to have no sins in their own eyes, but judge others who truly know that they are a sinner, and need to repent and turn to Jesus.

Those kinds of church folks are lost right in the church because of their eyes being full of darkness.

Let's you and me not be those kinds of church folks who carries themselves like they're the head of the church, trying to shake out someone who they believe to be a tare because they don't like him or her.

Only Jesus Christ is the head of the church because only Jesus is worthy to shake out who He knows to shake out of the church.

This is not because Jesus doesn't love that soul, who Jesus also loves no less than anyone else in the church.

There are those kinds of people who have a form of godliness, but deny the power of the Holy Spirit who they don't listen to when the Holy Spirit speaks to them through another brother or sister in the church.

There are those kinds of people who are not real with you and me, even in the church where many church folks have been hurt by so-called Christians who only appear to be real until you and I draw closer and closer to Jesus and begin to see the phoniness in them.

We Can Only Take

We can only take the choices that we made with us to the grave.

We can only take our character with us to the grave.

We can only take our destiny with us to the grave.

These three things are what God will judge us by in heaven where there is no death.

We can't take any money with us to the grave.

We can't spend any of it.

We can't take our vehicle with us to the grave where we can't drive it.

We can't take our house with us to the grave where we can't live in it.

All the choices that we make, good or bad, will go down in the grave with us one day.

All that we are is our true character that will go down in the grave with us one day.

The destiny that we make to be our own will go down in the grave with us one day.

All of this will happen to us if we are not alive when Jesus Christ comes back again because all who are in their graves right now have made their calling sure in Jesus Christ or made their calling sure in the devil.

All who have died in their mature right mind, Jesus will hold them accountable for knowing to do what is right and not doing it, thus making hell their destiny.

You and I can only take our choices and our character and our destiny with us to the grave where it will be too late to change from being evil, which can't enter into heaven when Jesus comes back again on the clouds of glory.

All the Good and Right that I Do

All the good and right that I do can't give me unspeakable joy, because only Jesus can give that to me.

All the good and right that I do can't esteem me who only Jesus can esteem for me to keep going on strong in Him.

All the good and right that I do can't lift me up like I am in heaven, only Jesus can do that because Jesus created the heavens.

All the good and right that I do can't take me safely through my trials, only Jesus can do that because I can only put my hope in Him and not in the good and right that I do.

All the good and right that I do can't give me peace of mind, only Jesus can do that because Jesus is the Prince of Peace to secure my mind in Him who overcame this troubled world thousands of years ago.

All the good and right that I do can't cleanse me of my sins, only Jesus can do that through His blood that was shed on the cross.

All the good and right that I do can't save me from my sins, only Jesus can do that because if I believe in Jesus, He will save me from my sins for repenting and turning to Him.

All the good and right that I do can't make me right with God, only Jesus can do that through His righteousness because my good and right is like filthy rags to God.

All the good and right that I do falls short of the glory of God because only Jesus had no sin in His flesh and only Jesus had pure motives and intentions and was always good and right.

I can deceive myself by thinking that always doing good and right in my own eyes is what I should do, but I can be mistaken and see what I think is good and right to do may be bad to God.

All the good and right that I do can't always be satisfying to please me, only Jesus Christ, my Lord and Savior, can please with His goodness that led me to repent and turn to a holy and righteous God who Jesus is One with and will sit on the right hand of God on His holy throne forever and ever.

All the good and right that I do can't heal my sin sick soul, only Jesus can heal me spiritually, which I need the most beyond mental, emotional and physical healing.

If I am healed spiritually in Jesus, then my soul is anchored in Jesus to take me to heaven when He comes back again.

All the good and right that I do can't take the place of Jesus who has brought me this far in my life beyond my mental, emotional, psychological and physical ills that the devil used for my bad when Jesus used it for my good and right for me to live my life unto Him today.

We Can't Do Anything About

We can't do anything about our pets getting old, which can sadden you and me to see our pets going through their body changes for the worst to one day die.

We can't do anything about getting old, no matter how many facelifts we can get — that won't stop us from getting old.

We can't do anything about the words that come out of someone's mouth — you and I have no control over taming anyone's tongue.

We can't do anything about the seasons that will change — the weather man and woman can only broadcast about those changes.

We can't do anything about what a day will bring — you and I have no control over the day and night and can't tell them what to bring us.

We can't do anything about tomorrow that may ask God to take you and me off of its schedule so we don't live to see tomorrow.

We can't do anything about what can happen in the next second that is not promised to you and me — we can get killed in a split second that can have our names written on it for only the Lord to erase in a split second.

We can't do anything about not being guilty before God — only Jesus Christ can represent our case and make us innocent before God through His righteousness to make you and me right with God if you and I believe in Jesus Christ.

We can't do anything about being born in sin and having a sinful nature to sin against God in our thoughts, words and actions — only the blood of Jesus can cleanse us of our sins if we ask Jesus to forgive us of our sins and believe in Him who can save us from our sins that we can't save ourselves from through our works in the church.

Has Been Around
for Thousands of Years

Spiritualism has been around for thousands of years, going way back to King Saul who went to see a witch to help him contact the prophet Samuel who was dead.

It was a demon disguising itself as the prophet Samuel who spoke to King Saul and led him to his fate.

Spiritualism is nothing new today, and there's a lot more spiritualism going on in this world from day to day as people are going to mediums to help them contact their dead loved ones.

The dead know nothing and the dead can't do anything, just like the bible says in the book of Ecclesiastes 9:5v (KJV).

Spiritualism will get more and more rampant in these last days as more and more people will be deceived by spiritualism, which is all about evil spirits impersonating the dead people from their graves.

You and I will not be deceived by spiritualism because we know the word of God tells us the truth about the dead knowing nothing and not being able to do anything in the grave.

It's the fallen angels from heaven disguising themselves as living human beings who are truly dead, and many people are talking to demons who deceive them into believing that they are talking to their loved ones who they believe to be in heaven looking down on them.

Spiritualism is of the devil who can disguise himself as an angel of light to cause many people to believe that spiritualism is of God who we can only worship in spirit and truth, but there is no truth in spiritualism.

Spiritualism has been in this world for thousands of years under the sun where spiritualism is limited and cannot enter into heaven, because no dead person can talk to you and me from heaven.

The Greatest Gift in the Church

The greatest gift in the church is love, and that's what everybody in the church needs the most.

The Lord didn't say that the greatest gift in the church is knowing the bible scriptures that are always good to know, but that can't top love.

The Lord didn't say that preaching is the greatest gift in the church even though preaching is always good for those who hear it and helps their faith grow strong in the Lord.

The greatest gift in the church is love, and that is what everybody in the church should want most.

The Lord didn't say that teaching is the greatest gift in the church, even though teaching is always good for everyone to learn more and more about Jesus Christ.

The Lord didn't say that the greatest gift in the church is singing, even though that is always good to meditate on in the church, but it can't lift anyone up in the church more than love.

The greatest gift in the church is love, which everybody needs the most while going through our trials and temptations.

The Lord didn't say that the greatest gift in the church is wisdom, even though it's always good for everyone in the church to make wise choices from day to day.

The Lord didn't say that healing is the greatest gift in the church, even though healing is always good for everyone in the church, especially when we're spiritually healed in our souls to keep us rooted and grounded in the Lord.

The greatest gift in the church is love, and everybody in the church needs love the most to be Jesus' disciples and go out into the world to feed His sheep with that love.

The Lord Jesus Christ didn't say that prosperity is the greatest gift in the church, even though prosperity is always good for us to help those who are less fortunate inside the church and outside the church.

The Lord didn't say that discernment is the greatest gift in the church, even though discernment is always good to help detect truth mixed with error that can creep into the church.

The greatest gift in the church is love, which everybody needs all the same to have no favoritism in the church.

The Lord didn't say that returning tithes and offerings is the greatest gift in the church, even though these are always good to return to the Lord to open up the windows of heaven and pour out blessings upon you and me who won't have room enough to receive them all from the Lord.

The Lord didn't say that being a leader is the greatest gift in the church, even though many leaders are always good to lead everyone closer and closer to Jesus Christ, who is the head of the church.

The greatest gift in the church is love, which everybody in the church should have for the Lord and for one another in a very deep way so the people of the world will see what they are truly missing out on for not giving Jesus a try after their backs are up against the hard walls of selfishness that love doesn't exist in at all from day to day.

The greatest gift in the church is love, and the Lord foreknew that there would be those church folks who would have a hard time loving everybody the same in the church.

The Lord foreknew that love would need to be the greatest gift in the church so everybody in the church could show the people of the world that we can't love God, who we don't see, and hate anyone who we do see inside the church and outside the church.

The greatest gift in the church is love, not anyone's ministry works that don't mean anything good at all in the church if you and I don't love one another deeply in the church with no favoritism.

The Lord didn't say that being a vegetarian is the greatest gift in the church, even though being a vegetarian is good for our bodies that are the temple of the Holy Spirit.

The Lord didn't say that giving gifts and awards to church folks is the greatest gift in the church.

The greatest gift in the church is love, which covers a multitude of sins inside and outside the church that needs God's love the most from day to day.

The Lord didn't say that me, myself and I are the greatest gift in the church, and no one's pride has ever loved the Lord Jesus Christ who is the head of the church.

The Lord didn't say that assembling ourselves together in the church is the greatest gift in the church that also has tares assembling together with the wheat in the church.

The greatest gift in the church is love which will accept all kinds of people in the church, no matter what bad things they did that the Lord will forgive us for and save us from our sins if we repent and turn to Him that we can only do in love for Him who has given the church the greatest gift.

The greatest gift in the church is not speaking in tongues, even though speaking different languages is always good to be a miraculous thing, especially to unbelievers to know that there is a true, living God.

I Miss Them So Very Much, O Lord

I miss my mother and stepdaughter so very much, O Lord, and I truly hope that they are saved in You, my Lord and Savior Jesus Christ, who I want to be saved in as I live and until I die.

My mother and my stepdaughter, as well as my first wife, passed away some years ago.

Especially my mother and my stepdaughter were so very dear to me because they loved me very much more than my deceased first wife, who was the mother of my stepdaughter.

My stepdaughter was like my blood daughter to me from her birth up to her young adult years.

My deceased first wife had a lot of problems and those problems caused a great deal of emotional pain to me and my stepdaughter.

I still shed some tears over my mother and stepdaughter, much more than I do over my deceased first wife, who I also loved and tried to give her my best.

I want to see them all again when Jesus Christ comes back again on the clouds of glory.

That will give me so much joy to go back to heaven, especially with my mother and stepdaughter, who I miss so very much.

I don't want to be lost and miss out on heaven and I don't want anyone I don't know to miss out on heaven either.

I truly hope that everyone I know in my life today loves Jesus like I love Jesus, who is the only One to save us all from our sins.

My greatest hope is to see all of my loved ones in heaven where there will be nothing but everlasting love that Jesus will give to you and me for loving Him and keeping His Commandments of love.

I don't want anyone to miss out on this, but everyone must choose to believe in Jesus Christ today and not put off it off.

There's Nothing Wrong About

There's nothing wrong about being rich, as long as you don't cheat the poor.

There's nothing wrong about being rich, as long as you don't rob the poor.

There's nothing wrong about being rich, as long as you don't put it above the Lord.

There's nothing wrong about getting a good education, as long as you don't use it for evil.

There's nothing wrong about getting a good education, as long as you don't get full of pride.

There's nothing wrong about getting a good education, as long as you don't put it above the Lord.

There's nothing wrong about looking good, as long as you don't use it to draw attention to yourself.

There's nothing wrong about looking good, as long as you don't put others down if they don't look good.

There's nothing wrong about looking good, as long as you don't put it above the Lord, who gave you good looks.

There's nothing wrong about having a lot of things, as long as you share them with those who don't have much.

There's nothing wrong about having a lot of things, as long as you use those things to help others who are less fortunate.

There's nothing wrong about having a lot of things, as long as you don't put them above the Lord, who owns everything in this world and up in heaven.

There's nothing wrong about not having yourself together sometimes, as long as you aren't too hard on yourself.

There's nothing wrong about not having yourself together sometimes, as long as you don't blame others for you not having yourself together.

There's nothing wrong about not having yourself together sometimes, as long as you don't' turn your back on Jesus Christ, who is perfect in all of His ways and can surely make you perfect before God in His righteousness.

An Abundance of Life

An abundance of life is praying without ceasing to our Lord and Savior Jesus Christ.

An abundance of life is studying the bible, both the old and new books, because they teach us to believe in Jesus Christ, who is the Son of God and the Light of the world.

An abundance of life is using our spiritual gifts to build up the church that Jesus Christ is the head of.

An abundance of life is surrendering our bodies so the Holy Spirit can dwell in us to be like Jesus Christ, who is all about eating healthy foods, drinking plenty of water, exercising and dressing in modest apparel.

An abundance of life is having a relationship with Jesus Christ.

An abundance of life is loving everyone, especially our brothers and sisters in the church where we assemble ourselves together to worship our Lord and Savior Jesus Christ.

An abundance of life is loving Jesus and keeping His Commandments day after day.

An abundance of life is giving testimonies about what Jesus brought us through.

An abundance of life is going through the fiery trials for Jesus' holy name sake.

An abundance of life is winning souls to Jesus Christ.

An abundance of life is living our lives unto our Lord and Savior Jesus Christ on our good days and bad days.

An abundance of life is Jesus cleansing us of our sins.

An abundance of life is Jesus forgiving us of our sins.

An abundance of life is confessing and repenting of our sins unto our Lord and Savior Jesus Christ.

An abundance of life is being saved in Jesus Christ.

An abundance of life is the Lord Jesus Christ opening the windows of heaven upon us for returning faithful tithes and offerings for the Lord to also pour out His blessings upon us that we don't have enough room to receive.

I Want to Walk
in Your Holy Spirit, O Lord

I want to walk in Your Holy Spirit, O Lord, because Your Holy Spirit convicts me of my sins for me to turn to You, my Lord, day after day.

I want to walk in Your Holy Spirit, O Lord, because Your Holy Spirit changed my life for me to be joyful about living for You, my Lord and Savior Jesus Christ.

I want to walk in Your Holy Spirit, O Lord, because Your Holy Spirit gives me spiritual gifts for me to edify the church to love You and Keep Your Commandments.

I want to walk in Your Holy Spirit, O Lord, because Your Holy Spirit teaches me all truth about You, my Lord and Savior Jesus Christ.

I want to walk in Your Holy Spirit, O Lord, because Your Holy Spirit fills me up with love, joy, peace, temperance, patience, kindness, gentleness, faithfulness and goodness.

I want to walk in Your Holy Spirit and not walk in lust, envy, jealousy, greed, pride hatred, covetousness and selfishness.

I want to walk in Your Holy Spirit day after day, O Lord, so that your Holy Spirit can comfort my soul and help me to deny myself and pick up my cross and follow You, my Lord Jesus Christ, from day to day.

Sometimes When I

Sometimes when I think that I am so right, I am so wrong.

Sometimes when I say something that I believe to be right, I am so wrong.

Sometimes when I do something that I believe to be right to do, I am so wrong.

Sometimes I am just downright so wrong about what I think.

Sometimes I am just downright so wrong about what I say.

Sometimes I am just downright so wrong about what I do.

I was born in sin to have a sinful nature and sometimes be so wrong, and just because I'm a Christian doesn't keep me from falling short of the glory of God.

No matter how much I think right, I will sometimes think wrong.

No matter how much I talk right, I will sometimes talk wrong.

No matter how much I do right, I will sometimes do wrong.

It's truly Jesus giving me His Holy Spirit to help me to think right.

It's truly Jesus giving me His Holy Spirit to help me to talk right.

It's truly Jesus giving me His Holy Spirit to help me to do right.

Sometimes when I think I am looking at something good, I am so wrong.

Sometimes when I believe I am listening to something good, I am so wrong.

Sometimes when I believe I am holding something good in my hands, I am so wrong.

No matter how many good choices I make, sometimes I am so wrong.

All the time I can choose to listen to the Holy Spirit who can help me to be so right.

Sometimes when I am so wrong, I can choose to obey the Holy Spirit speaking to me to do so right unto the Lord Jesus Christ.

The Side Effect of Life

The good side effect of life is treating people right.

The bad side effect of life is hating people.

The good side effect of life is giving something good to people.

The bad side effect of life is stealing from people.

The good side effect of life is helping people.

The bad side effect of life is harming people.

The good side effect of life is loving people.

The bad side effect of life is killing people.

The good side effect of life is encouraging people.

The bad side effect of life is putting people down.

The good side effect of life is being happy for people.

The bad side effect of life is being envious of people.

The good side effect of life is giving people justice.

The bad side effect of life is falsely accusing people.

The good side effect of life is being at peace with people.

The bad side effect of life is making trouble for people.

The good side effect of life is telling people the truth.

The bad side effect of life is telling people lies.

The good side effect of life is taking our time to do something.

The bad side effect of life is doing something in a hurry without thinking.

The good side effect of life is not being opinionated about someone.

The bad side effect of life is judging someone.

The good side effect of life is taking good care of yourself.

The bad side effect of life is letting yourself go.

The good side effect of life is believing in Jesus Christ.

The bad side effect of life is rejecting Jesus.

The good side effect of life is loving Jesus and keeping His holy law.

The bad side effect of life is rebelling against Jesus.

The good side effect of life is to repent and turn to Jesus.

The bad side effect of life is holding onto unconfessed sins.

The good side effect of life is being a new creature in Jesus Christ.

The bad side effect of life is being that old carnal-minded creature.

The good side effect of life is being cleansed of our sins in the blood of Jesus.

The bad side effect of life is living in our sins.

The good side effect of life is being saved in Jesus Christ.

The bad side effect of life is being lost in our sins.

The doctor's medicine can give us some bad side effects.

No one can say that the good spiritual medicine of God's holy word has a bad side effect on them, because there are no bad side effects in the bible that tells us all about Jesus Christ who is the greatest doctor, surgeon and nurse to heal our sin-sick souls.

There are People Who

There are people who only love to talk about how they feel and what they are going through.

There are people who don't care anything about how you feel and what you are going through.

There are people who will complain about everything and how everything is a big deal to them.

There are people who want you to listen to what they have to say but they really don't want to listen to what you have to say.

There are people who only see what they say as being important but they don't think that anything you say has any importance to them.

There are people who act like they are the only ones having it hard in life and they could care less if you are having it hard in life too.

There are people who act like this world revolves around them and they don't care if you live in this world just like them.

There are people who will only see and talk about bad things in this world and they don't really care to see and talk about the good things in this world.

There are church folks who are so full of themselves and they won't compliment you on anything good that you do.

There are church folks who love to talk about the wrongs they see in people but they don't care to talk about the right things that people do.

There are church folks who see themselves as perfect in their own eyes and will criticize others over everything they see to be wrong about that those other people do.

There are church folks who will carry themselves like they are self-made and will claim to own something but they will not acknowledge with you that the Lord owns all things and lives forever beyond the grave that many church folks seem to forget they will meet one day and they won't be able to take anything with them to their grave.

Jesus Can

Some things can be too hard for you and me, but there is nothing too hard for Jesus.

Some things can be impossible for you and me, but there is nothing impossible for Jesus.

There are some things that you and I can't do, but Jesus can do all things.

Jesus can sing songs that the angels can't sing.

Jesus can go to places where the angels can't go.

Jesus can do things that the angels can't do.

Jesus can speak words that the angels can't speak.

Some things can be too hard for the angels, but there is nothing too hard for Jesus.

Some things can be impossible for the angels, but there is nothing impossible for Jesus.

If we make it to heaven when Jesus comes back again on the clouds of glory, we will be immortal like Jesus, but only Jesus is self-existing.

Some things can be too hard for you and me, but only Jesus can make our burdens as light as a feather.

Some things can be impossible for you and me, but Jesus can speak to the impossible that will obey Jesus and become possible to you and me.

Jesus can do all things but fail, and the angels in heaven forever know that better than you and me because they are still in heaven for believing that Lucifer didn't stand a chance to defeat Jesus in the war in heaven.

We Can Want to Rush

We can want to rush a second that will obey the Lord and wait on you and me in one second to make the right choice that may be a matter of our life or death.

Maybe in a matter of our life or death we can want to rush a minute that will obey the Lord and wait on you and me to say the right words to encourage someone to live for the Lord.

We can want to rush an hour that will obey the Lord and wait on you and me to do the right thing to help someone else do what is right.

We can want to rush a day that will obey the Lord to wait on you and me to slow down.

We can want to rush the week that will obey the Lord and wait on you and me to learn from our mistakes.

We can want to rush the month that will obey the Lord and wait on you and me to admit our wrongdoings.

We can want to rush the year that will obey the Lord and wait on you and me to confess and repent of our sins that we can believe don't exist in us, especially if we're doing good things.

We can want to rush the present that will obey the Lord and wait on you and me to put all of our trust in the Lord.

We can want to rush the future that will obey the Lord and wait on you and me to be prepared to stand up for Jesus, even if everything is taken away from you and me who can want to rush Jesus to come back again and not want to wait on souls to repent and turn to Jesus before it's too late.

Being Real

If I'm not being real with you and if you aren't being real with me, then how can we be real with Jesus who was real with everyone when He lived in this world with no sin in his flesh.

You and I can go to church all that we want to, but if I'm not being real with you about how I'm so messed up without Jesus, then I'm being a phony right in the church.

It's the same for you, because you'd be a phony if you are not being real with me about how you are messed up without Jesus.

There are people who can't handle you and me being real with them, especially about how we lived our lives before we repented of our sins and turned to Jesus.

If you and I are afraid about being real with one another about our weaknesses that we need to pray about over one another, then why waste Jesus' time to save us from our sins?

If we are not being real in loving Jesus and keeping His Commandments, then that is real death because the wages of sin is death upon all.

Jesus is always real with you and me, because His love for us is forever real.

Jesus will forgive us of our sins, cleanse us of our sins and save us from our sins if we are being real about confessing our sins and repenting of our sins and turning to Jesus every day.

Once we are saved doesn't mean that we are always saved, we must do this every day.

There are people who are afraid about being real because they know that there are many judgmental people who will have certain opinions about them for being real.

So far, I've never heard about anyone dropping dead over someone being real with them, because being real won't kill anyone who loves being real, especially about doing God's holy will.

There are people who will be more willing to believe that a ghost is real to talk to, but they won't want to talk to you and me, who are real flesh and blood for them to touch and know that we are real, because we're being real with them about the Lord.

Jesus proved to Thomas that He was real and not a ghost, that is not real and won't be real with you and me about the truth.

A ghost doesn't have a real body, but is surely real evil and is only a fallen angel from heaven that is eternally real.

I Will Know and They Will Know

There have been people in my life who did me so wrong, but if I make it to heaven and see them there, I will know that they repented of their sins and lived for Jesus and I will be glad to see them in heaven.

I did some people wrong in their lives, but if they make it to heaven and see me there, they will know that I repented of my sins and lived for Jesus and they will be glad to see me in heaven.

Heaven is a great and wonderful place where we will be glad to be and glad to see even those who lied on us, stole from us, abused us, cheated on us and even may have killed us.

We will be glad to see even those people in heaven because we will know right away that they confessed all of their sins and repented of all their sins to be there in heaven with Jesus Christ, just like you and me.

Jesus is coming back again to take all who love and obey Him to heaven.

I will know that I made it to heaven for turning to Jesus every day that I lived, beyond all of my mistakes that caused me to hurt myself the most, even more than hurting others.

Even those I hurt will be glad to see me in heaven because they will know that I repented and turned to Jesus before it was too late.

I will be glad to see those in heaven who hurt me and I will embrace them because they repented and turned to Jesus before it was too late.

If I make it to heaven and especially see all of those I know I will be glad to see them all, no matter if many of them were my enemies in the past because I will know without a doubt that they made their hearts right with Jesus, just like me who they will be glad to see too.

Heaven is an eternal place of love, peace and gladness for all the holy saints to be like Jesus, who will be glad to take you and me to heaven when He comes back again on the clouds of glory.

If I make it to heaven and see you there, I will be glad that you made it to heaven and you will be glad that I made it to heaven if you see me there.

We both will surely know that we both loved Jesus with all our minds, hearts, souls and strength if we see each other in heaven.

If we see each other in heaven, we will know we have moved beyond the dark times when we were not very sure about our calling in Jesus who calls everyone to repent and turn to Him before it's too late.

The Righteous and the Wicked Alike

The righteous and the wicked alike must drink water and eat food to live.

The righteous and the wicked alike have a mind to think and a heart to feel.

The righteous and the wicked alike will get married and have some children.

The righteous and the wicked alike will have some disagreements.

The righteous and the wicked alike will get sick sooner or later.

The righteous and the wicked alike will look in the mirror to see how they look.

The righteous and the wicked alike need to take a shower.

The righteous and the wicked alike need to brush their teeth.

The righteous and the wicked alike need a job.

The righteous and the wicked alike will have dreams in their sleep during the night.

The righteous and the wicked alike will make plans.

The righteous and the wicked alike need clothes to wear.

The righteous and the wicked alike need shoes on their feet.

The righteous and the wicked alike will talk to someone.

The righteous and the wicked alike need a house to live in.

The righteous and the wicked alike will see the rain falling from the sky.

The righteous and the wicked alike have a limit to not go over.

The righteous and the wicked have something in common and that's the free will to choose.

The righteous and the wicked alike will die

The righteous and the wicked alike will see Jesus on the clouds of glory when the righteous living will be changed from mortal to immortality while the wicked living will drop dead at the brightness of Jesus' eternal light.

The righteous and the wicked have a judge over them to judge their deeds fairly to seal their destiny that the righteous and the wicked will choose in the land of the living.

We Can't Get Ahead of God

Abraham's wife, Sahar, tried to get ahead of God by telling her husband, Abraham, to sleep with her slave, Hagar, to get her pregnant.

Sahar could not get pregnant at that time, because it wasn't God's time for her to get pregnant with a son to be blessed by God.

If Sahar could not get ahead of God, then who are you and I to get ahead of God who we can't ever get ahead of and be right about it?

There is nothing right about trying to get ahead of God, because we will surely just mess things up by trying to get ahead of God like Sahar, who messed things up and regretted it.

We can't get ahead of God who is always on time to give us what we need.

God knows all about what we need even before we get down on our knees and pray to Him about our needs and some of our wants.

God will give these to us if what we want is in His holy will.

Sahar caused her Egyptian slave to suffer in some ways because Sahar tried to get ahead of God, but she failed to do this at the age of seventy-six years old.

Abraham was eighty-six years old when he was also the husband of his wife Hagar, who Sahar wanted him to marry before he slept with her.

The Lord God let Sahar know that her time was not his time, which was fourteen years later for Sahar to get pregnant at the age of ninety years old.

God blessed Sahar to give birth to a son who would love God with all his heart.

We should learn from Sahar's mistake and wait on God to work out everything for our good, because we can't do that on our own time.

Sahar tried to get ahead of God to do things her way and not wait on God who is perfect in all of His ways of doing things on time beyond our time that is not always on time.

You and I can't get ahead of God and will surely waste our time trying, just like Sahar wasted her time and had to learn the hard way that it's always good to wait on God who causes no one to regret waiting on Him.

Don't Believe that You Can

Don't believe that you can pick up a poisonous snake and not get bit.

Don't believe that you can walk in front of a speeding car and not get hit.

Don't believe that you can eat spoiled food and not get sick.

Don't believe that you can jump off a high building and not break any bones.

Don't believe that you can pull a dog's tail and not get bit.

Don't believe that you can tell a lie and not get caught.

Don't believe that you can make good grades in school without studying.

Don't believe that you can get a college degree without graduating.

Don't believe that you can eat a lot of food without gaining any weight.

Don't believe that you can talk a lot and also be a good listener at the same time.

Don't believe that you can put your hand in the fire and not get burned.

Don't believe that you can talk to the same person every day and not get attached to them.

Don't believe that you can drive safe on the road and not get into an accident.

Don't believe that you can sin against the Lord and not be wrong.

Don't believe that you can hear a sermon in church and not be affected by it in some kind of way.

Don't believe that you love Jesus without loving your neighbors.

Don't believe that you can be wise and not fear God and keep His Commandments.

Don't believe that you can pray to God without the Holy Spirit making your prayers make good sense to God.

Don't believe that you can live for Jesus without repenting of your sins.

Don't believe that you can be saved when you don't believe in Jesus Christ.

Don't believe that you can go to heaven without Jesus coming back again on the clouds of glory.

Don't believe that you can live right by example without living by the word of God.

Don't believe that you can know who God is when you don't know His holy word.

Don't believe that you can do the Lord's will without listening to and obeying the voice of His Holy Spirit speaking all the truth of God to you and me.

Tell it to unbelievers in love and without condemnation because the truth of God is His holy word that you and I should always speak to everyone in love.

Don't believe that you can be like Jesus if you don't hate sin that was originated by the devil who loves to tempt you and me to sin against God in seen and unseen ways every day.

Don't believe that you can defeat the devil without having Jesus on your side to make the devil tremble and flee from you and me to get the victory in Jesus.

Sin is Sin in the Presence of God

Sin is sin in the presence of God, whether the sin is educated or illiterate.

Sin is sin in the presence of God, whether the sin is smart or dumb.

Sin is sin in the presence of God, whether the sin is rich, upper middle class, middle class, lower middle class or poor.

Sin is sin in the presence of God, whether the sin is out in the open or in secrecy.

Sin is sin in the presence of God, whether the sin is knowledgeable or ignorant.

Sin is sin in the presence of God, whether the sin is polished up or smeared up.

Sin is sin in the presence of God, whether the sin is loud or quiet.

Sin is sin in the presence of God, whether the sin is bold or fearful.

Sin is sin in the presence of God, whether the sin is direct or indirect.

Sin is sin in the presence of God, whether the sin is slick or sly.

Sin is sin in the presence of God, whether the sin is attractive or unattractive.

Sin is sin in the presence of God, whether the sin is genius or stupid.

Sin is sin in the presence of God, whether the sin is a sinful thought or sinful words or a sinful action that only Jesus never possessed in his life here on earth to save us from our sins and renew our lives before God like we never sinned against God.

The Devil Has Deceived So Many People

The devil has deceived so many people and made them believe that going to church is a big waste of their time because they see hypocrites in the church not being like Jesus.

The devil has deceived so many people and made them believe that Jesus is not real because they don't see many people in the church being real about loving Jesus and keeping His Commandments.

The devil has deceived so many people and made them believe that worshipping Jesus is no good thing for them to do because they see church folks worshipping material things.

The devil has deceived so many people and made them believe that Jesus is a fairy tale because they see so many church folks living their lives like an imaginary cartoon character.

The devil has deceived so many people and made them believe that many church folks have lost their minds because they see many church folks not living what they talk about Jesus that flows from their minds with no actions to back them up and make them like Jesus.

The devil has deceived so many people and made them believe there is no God because seeing many church folks carrying themselves like they made themselves prosperous and leave God off the tips of their tongues because they speak no praises unto God for their achievements in life.

The devil has deceived so many people in this world because they see many church folks with a war face pushing them away from wanting to step foot inside any church.

The devil has deceived so many people in this world and made them believe that real, true Christians are delusional because they believe in a God they don't see, so they make their gods to be seen but they are only temporary and are powerless to convict anyone's consciousness to make the right destiny choice before it's too late.

Only Here on Earth

Only here on earth are many people afraid to get close to one another.

Only here on earth are many people afraid to trust one another.

Only here on earth did sin originate fear in the human race and in the animals.

Only here on earth are many people afraid to love one another.

Only here on earth do many people believe it's a good thing to be prejudiced against anyone who doesn't look like them.

Only here on earth will many people teach their children to hate anyone who doesn't look like them.

Only here on earth can the devil possess anyone to lean to their own ways of living like they want from day to day.

Only here on earth does time exist for everybody to live their moment in time unto the Lord Jesus Christ.

Only here on earth does sin exist to cause many people to go to war against one another over wanting things that they don't have the right to own.

Only here on earth is where the Son of God came to become like one of us but without sin to redeem us back to God.

Only here on earth does sin separate us from God because you and I were born in sin to have sin even in our hereditary tendencies to sin against God so unaware.

Only here on earth was the church originated by Jesus Christ, who is the head of the church, not any human being who was born in sin that would corrupt the church with truth mixed with error.

Only here on earth will God set up His headquarters for all the other worlds to surround and worship God with all the holy saints in the new earth below the new heavens that God will create.

Only here on earth does a second chance still exist because the Lord gives everyone a second chance to repent and turn to Him before it's too late.

That second chance applies to everybody who is mature and in their right mind to know right from wrong.

Babies and immature children and those with mental deficiencies are not held accountable to God.

Only here on earth did Jesus, Himself, became sin on the cross to save even the uttermost sinners, which is everybody because we are all born in sin.

Jesus gave up His life on the cross and rose from the grave to back up all that He did for us to receive eternal life for believing in Him.

O Lord, You Created Everybody Different

O Lord, You created everybody different in some kind of way because even twins are different in some kind of way.

Everybody will not eat all the same foods.

Everybody will not say all the same words.

Everybody will not have all the same dreams.

Everybody will not do all the same things.

Everybody will not know all the same things.

Everybody will not watch all the same TV programs.

Everybody will not go to college.

Everybody will not be a genius.

Everybody will not be on time.

Everybody will not be rich.

Everybody will not be poor.

Everybody will not be a good talker.

Everybody will not be a good listener.

Everybody will not be a doctor.

Everybody will not be a lawyer.

Everybody will not be a poet.

Everybody will not be an author.

Everybody will not be a publisher.

Everybody will not be a nurse.

Everybody will not be a psychiatrist.

Everybody will not get married.

Everybody will not be a criminal.

Everybody will not be a teacher.

Everybody will not be a preacher.

Everybody will not be a soldier.

Everybody will not be a movie star.

Everybody will not be a singer.

Everybody will not be a pilot.

Everybody will not be a dentist.

Everybody will not own a business.

Everybody will not have a pet.

Everybody will not be a judge.

Everybody will not be a truck driver.

Everybody will not be an engineer.

O Lord, You created everybody different in some kind of way, but no matter how different everyone is You give Your salvation to everybody to be saved in You, O Lord.

Everybody will not be a quick learner.

Everybody will not be a quick thinker.

Everybody will not be educated.

Everybody in the church will not have all the same spiritual gifts.

Everybody in the church will not have all the same faith in the Lord.

Everybody in the church will not have all the same growth in the Lord.

Everybody in the church will not have all the same testimonies about what the Lord brought us through.

O Lord, You created everybody different in the church where everybody is one body in You who are the head of the church that you gave different body parts to in order to win souls to You.

Overlook

You and I can surely overlook some things that we can regret in more ways than one.

You and I can believe that we didn't overlook something small that could become a big thing if we truly need it.

You and I can surely overlook something that we need to have to make things much better for us.

You and I can surely overlook something that we need to use to make things easy for us day after day.

The Lord is always so merciful on you and me after we overlook something that we need; the Lord will give it to us, especially if we love and obey the Lord.

The Lord will not overlook our smallest problems that He surely knows would become big problems if He leaves them to us to work out on our own because we would make our problems so much worse.

You and I can surely overlook even our own soul's salvation in some ways that we don't see because we can be so into how many bible scriptures we can quote and how many things we can do in the church that have no salvation to give to us.

Jesus will never overlook anyone's soul's salvation, no matter how many times everyone overlooks something that is needed in their own lives.

You and I were born in sin to overlook something that we can forget to say and do that can even cause us to lose our lives.

Jesus will surely overlook anyone's sins through true repentance and turning to Him.

The Mind is Very Powerful

We make our choices with our minds every day that our thoughts come from our minds.

Whatever we think about comes from our minds.

We can think to say good words or bad words.

The mind is very powerful and takes us from words into actions and also puts thoughts into words every day that the mind is the path to life or death.

The mind is very powerful and can create good ideas or bad ideas.

The mind is very powerful and creates reasons and gives us an imagination.

The mind is very powerful and creates fantasies, illusions, finds fault and tells lies.

The mind is very powerful and can create positivity or negativity.

The mind is very powerful and can create agreements or disagreements.

The mind is very powerful and can create encouragement or discouragement.

Every word that we say comes from our minds.

Every choice we make comes from our minds.

The mind is very powerful every day and can make our hearts change for better or for worse.

Our thoughts come from our minds and can enter into our hearts to cause us to feel good or bad.

Our words come from our minds and can enter into our hearts to cause us to feel bold or afraid.

Our choices come from our minds and can enter into our hearts to cause us to feel great or feel like nothing.

The mind is very powerful every day.

Our minds can make us feel like we're in a torture chamber or like a bird flying so free up in the sky.

The mind is very powerful and can be filled with the choices we make, but the mind that is stayed on Jesus Christ will think on honest things, lovely things, pure things, true things, and just things.

The mind is very powerful every day, and like the bible says: "Thou wilt keep him in perfect peace, whose mind is stayed on thee: because he trusteth in thee."

Isaiah 26:3v
Philippians 4:8v

It Doesn't Take Much Effort

It doesn't take much effort to sin against You, O Lord, in thoughts, words and actions.

O Lord, it doesn't take much effort for me to pull away from you in my thoughts that can easily go into dark places that only Your Holy Spirit can bring me back from when thinking about You, O Lord.

It doesn't take much effort for me to say sinful words that take my heart into dark places, O Lord, but then Your Holy Spirit speaks to me and tells me to come back into the light of God's holy word and live by it.

The Holy Spirit will help me to do that if I ask You to forgive me of my sins.

It doesn't take much effort at all to sin against You, O Lord, because I was born in sin to be in my hereditary tendencies and in my genes and this allows me to easily do something wrong.

Your Holy Spirit will easily bring me back to You, O Lord, if I was to listen to and obey the voice of Your Holy Spirit telling me so kindly to repent and turn back to You, O Lord.

It doesn't take much effort at all to desire sinful living, regardless of how long I have been going to church where I need Your Holy Spirit, O Lord, to dwell in me because the devil goes to church too and can cause me to sin against You, O Lord, in the church that You, O Lord Jesus Christ, are the head of.

You, O Lord, bring me back to You through Your holy word that can surely light up the dark places in my life so that I can live for You, O Lord, inside and outside the church.

There is Only One Salvation

There are many different religious groups of people, but there is only one salvation and that is in Jesus Christ, who we must believe in to be saved.

There is only one salvation and that is not in the Catholic church, but only in Jesus Christ, who we must believe in to be saved.

There is only one salvation and that is not in the Baptist church, but only in Jesus Christ, who we must believe in to be saved.

There is only one salvation and that is not in the Methodist church, but only in Jesus Christ, who we must believe in to be saved.

There is only one salvation and that is not in the Mormon church, but only in Jesus Christ, who we must believe in to be saved.

There is only one salvation and that is not in the Jehovah's Witness church, but only in Jesus Christ, who we must believe in to be saved.

There is only one salvation and that is not in the Holiness church, but only in Jesus Christ, who we must believe in to be saved.

There is only one salvation and that is not in the Muslim religion, but only in Jesus Christ, who we must believe in to be saved.

There is only one salvation and that is not in the Seventh Day Adventist church, but only in Jesus Christ, who we must believe in to be saved.

There is only one salvation and that is not in the Hindu religion, but only in Jesus Christ, who we must believe in to be saved.

There is only one salvation and that is not in the Buddhist religion, but only in Jesus Christ, who we must believe in to be saved.

There is only one salvation for all men to be saved, and that is only in Jesus Christ and not in any church or religion because they cannot save us from our sins.

Only Jesus Christ can cleanse us and save us from our sins if we believe in Him.

Many people will be lost in every church and in every religion for not believing in Jesus Christ and only believing in their church ministries and religious ceremonies that have no salvation.

Salvation is only in Jesus Christ, who is the origin of salvation for all men.

Only Jesus Christ, our Lord and Savior, can forgive us of our sins, cleanse us of our sins and save us from our sins if we confess our sins and repent and turn to Him and believe in Him.

There is only one salvation that is given to all human beings and only Jesus Christ can give us that salvation.

Salvation does not come from ourselves, no matter how religious and perfect our church attendance is from birth to old age.

Salvation is not in anyone's spiritual gifts and great knowledge of the bible, and it is not in anyone's good and right actions that can't save anyone from their sins.

Only Jesus Christ can save us from our sins.

There is only one salvation and it is not in anyone or anything that we see in this world.

Only Jesus Christ can give us salvation for believing in Him for as long as we live.

Only Jesus can orchestrate it so that all human beings can be saved in Him before it's too late, as long as we humans freely choose to accept the salvation that Jesus freely gives to us all to be saved in Him.

Will Worship

Many people in this world will worship who and what they can see.

Many people will not worship what they can't see from day to day.

We can't see the true and only living Son of God.

There was a time back in the bible days that many people did see the Son of God talking to them, feeding them, healing them and casting demons out of them.

Many of those people refused to worship Jesus Christ, and that made many of them more worse off than many people today who can't see Jesus and don't want to worship Him because of that.

It's so easy to want to worship the things we see from day to day, and material things will look so good in our eyesight.

Many people in this world love to worship who they can see and the material things in their lives they want to be their idol gods.

There may be over a thousand idol gods that many people in this world can worship from day to day.

The idol gods will increase more and more in the eyes of many people in these last days, but only the true, living Son of God who is coming back again on the clouds of glory with all the angels in heaven worshipping Him is worthy to be worshipped in heaven and on earth forever and ever.

Jesus is not only the Son of God, but Jesus is God who was made flesh.

Many people didn't see Jesus to be worthy of worship when he was on earth.

Many people in this world will worship themselves like they're gods because they believe they made themselves geniuses, rich or powerful; but these are things the true, living God blessed them with.

Even worse than them are the many poor people who will worship themselves like gods, especially if they have great athletic talents and get rich from them.

They feel so proud and believe they made themselves, like they self-exist before God, who is the only self-existing God.

Many people in this world from the beginning of time going down to the end of time in this world will worship false gods and find that so easy to do from day to day.

Many people in the church will worship their knowledge of the bible and their spiritual gifts and church positions as if Jesus Christ doesn't exist in the church and isn't the head of the church.

There is So Much Stuff

There is so much mental stuff going on in many people's minds every day.

There is so much emotional stuff going on in many people's hearts every day.

There is so much evil stuff going on in many people's minds every day.

There is so much evil stuff going on in many people's hearts every day.

There is so much confusing stuff going on in many people's minds every day.

There is so much delusional stuff going on in many people's minds every day.

There is so much unstable stuff going on in many people's minds every day.

There is so much deadly stuff going on in many people's minds every day.

There is so much troubling stuff going on in many people's hearts every day.

There is so much messed up stuff going on in many people's hearts every day.

There is so much sinful stuff going on in many people's hearts every day.

There is so much spiritual stuff going on every day in a real, true Christian's mind and heart and life that only the spiritual stuff is always good stuff to bless our souls for us to be like Jesus.

The Only Way

The only way that another second is promised to me is in the Lord's will and not my will.

The only way that another minute is promised to me is in the Lord's will and not my will.

The only way that another hour is promised to me is in the Lord's will and not my will.

The only way that all of today is promised to me is in the Lord's will and not my will.

The only way that another day is promised to me is in the Lord's will and not my will.

The only way that all of this week is promised to me is in the Lord's will and not my will.

The only way that another week is promised to me is in the Lord's will and not my will.

The only way that all of this month is promised to me is in the Lord's will and not my will.

The only way that another month is promised to me is in the Lord's will and not my will.

The only way that all of this year is promised to me is in the Lord's will and not my will.

The only way that another year is promised to me is in the Lord's will and not my will.

The only way that my eyesight is promised to me is in the Lord's will and not my will.

The only way that my hearing is promised to me is in the Lord's will and not my will.

The only way that the strength in my body will not leave me is in the Lord's will and not my will.

The only way that my voice won't leave me is in the Lord's will and not my will.

The only way I can move around here and there is in the Lord's will and not in my will.

The only way I can achieve anything is in the Lord's will and not in my will.

The only way that my health won't fail me is in the Lord's will and not in my will.

The only way I can do anything good is in the Lord's will and not in my will.

The only way for all of my well-being is in the Lord's will and not in my will.

The only way I can make good choices is in the Lord's will and not in my will that has caused me to make bad choices.

The only way I can live is doing the Lord's will and not my will that will surely shorten my life.

The only way that I can die and live again in the afterlife is to do the Lord's will that He is coming back again to take me to heaven that is in the Lord's will if I am saved in Him.

The only way for anyone to be a real, true Christian is to do the Lord's will, which is keeping His Commandments of love for God and our neighbors, but doing our own will is breaking God's holy law.

I Feel Like I was Right There

When I read the bible, I feel like I was right there with Adam and Eve in the Garden of Eden.

When I read the bible, I feel like I was right there with Noah and his family in the ark.

When I read the bible, I feel like I was right there with Abraham, Sarah and Isaac.

When I read the bible, I feel like I was right there with Lot and his wife and daughters.

When I read the bible, I feel like I was right there with Hagar and her son Ishmael.

When I read the bible, I feel like I was right there with Joseph who was thrown down in a pit.

When I read the bible, I feel like I was right there when Jacob had to wrestle with God.

When I read the bible, I feel like I was right there with Moses up on Mount Sinai where God appeared before Moses in a burning bush.

When I read the bible, I feel like I was right there with Rahab who hid the spies.

When I read the bible, I feel like I was right there with Joshua and his army marching around the walls of Jericho seven times before the walls fell down.

When I read the bible, I feel like I was right there with Elijah on Mount Carmel where he challenged the prophets of Baal for a showdown of the true, living God against the false gods of Baal.

When I read the bible, I feel like I was right there with David who faced Goliath and killed him with a stone charging out of sling in the name of the Lord.

When I read the bible, I feel like I was right there with Ester who was crowned queen next to King Xerxes.

When I read the bible, I feel like I was right there with Jonah in the belly of the whale for disobeying God.

When I read the bible, I feel like I was right there with Ezekiel down in the valley of dry bones where the hand of the Lord was upon him to call the dry bones back to life.

When I read the bible, I feel like I was right there with Jesus who was born in a manger.

When I read the bible, I feel like I was right there with Mary who was the mother of a God made flesh in her womb.

When I read the bible, I feel like I was right there with Jesus feeding thousands of people with bread and fish from heaven that He multiplied from only a few fish and bread from a basket.

When I read the bible, I feel like I was right there with Jesus healing the sick, casting out demons, opening the eyes of the blind and raising the dead.

When I read the bible, I feel like I was right there with Jesus being beaten and crucified on the cross in the eyesight of many unbelievers who made fun of Him and taunted him about coming down off the cross, which He could have done but then we wouldn't all be here today if he had come down off that cross.

When I read the bible, I feel like I was right there with Peter who denied Jesus three times before unbelievers because he was afraid that he would be killed for claiming to be one of Jesus' disciples.

When I read the bible, I feel like I was right there with Judas betraying Jesus for thirty pieces of silver.

When I read the bible, I feel like I was right there with Mary Magdalene telling the disciples that she spoke to Jesus who had risen from the dead.

When I read the bible, I feel like I was right there with the disciples who Jesus appeared to for doubting Thomas to touch Him and know that Jesus was alive.

When I read the bible, I feel like I was right there with Jesus who ascended back up to heaven before His disciples so they would know he will come back again the same way He left them: looking up in the sky and gazing with amazement upon Jesus Christ, the Lord of lords and King of kings.

When I read the bible, I feel like I was right there with Jesus who is the origin of all life and revealed all life to you and me in the bible that also tells us about other worlds that Jesus created.

The bible tells us about the sons of God from other worlds standing before God as the devil represents this world to try to convince God that Job is not who God knew Job to be about him in the earth where God also originated the bible.

A Big Heart

If you and I have a big heart and don't want to kill any animals, then we should have a bigger heart and not want to kill any human being who God created in His image.

If you and I have a big heart and want to take good care of our pets, then we should have a bigger heart and want to take good care of any human being who God created in His image.

If you and I spend money on buying food for our pets, then we can surely give some money to the homeless and not question them about what they need the money for.

If you and I have a big heart and feel bad about killing an animal while driving down the road, then we should have a bigger heart and drive safely so we don't cause an accident that can kill other human beings driving down the road.

If you and I have a big heart and want to keep our pets safe from harm and danger, then we should have a bigger heart and want to keep our families safe from harm and danger.

If you and I have a big heart and don't want to treat any animal badly, then we should have a bigger heart and not want to treat any human being badly because every human being is created in the image of God.

If you and I have a big heart and want to see an animal get well after being sick, then we should have a bigger heart and want to see a human being get well from a sickness.

If you and I have a big heart and want to see our pets live a long life, then we should have a bigger heart and want to see a human being live a long life, especially doing the Lord's will.

If you and I have a big heart and want to see a turtle make its way safely across the dangerous highway, then we should have a bigger heart and want to see a human being get to where he is going while walking or riding a bike on the side of the highway or local road.

If you and I can have a big heart for animals who God can speak through like God spoke through the donkey to warn Balaam, then we should have a bigger heart for human beings who take heed of God warning them to believe in His Son, Jesus Christ.

If you and I have a big heart for our pets and them to make it to heaven, then we should have a bigger heart for human beings to make it to heaven for believing in Jesus Christ who is coming back again on the clouds of glory to take all of his children to heaven and hopefully good animals too.

Spiritually Charged Up

You and I need to get spiritually charged up in Jesus Christ every day, because you and I can't afford to let our spiritual batteries get low or go dead.

We will get spiritually charged up in Jesus Christ if we read our bible every day and live by what it says.

We will get spiritually charged up in Jesus Christ by praying to Jesus every day and ask Him to give us His Holy Spirit.

We will get spiritually charged up in Jesus Christ by trusting Jesus to carry us through our trials.

We will get spiritually charged up in Jesus Christ by denying ourselves and picking up our crosses to follow Jesus Christ through the good days and bad days.

We will get spiritually charged up in Jesus Christ by loving Jesus and keeping all ten of His Commandments.

We will get spiritually charged up in Jesus Christ by assembling ourselves together in the church to worship Jesus, especially on His holy Sabbath day of rest.

The only way that you and I can keep our spiritual batteries charged up is by doing the Lord's will, because if we do our own will our spiritual batteries will surely get very low and sooner or later go dead and you and I will have no power to resist the temptations of the devil.

Jesus is our only power source and He charges you and me up spiritually every day, because a dead spiritual battery is of no good use to anyone.

There are People Who Believe

There are people who believe they can talk to the Lord any kind of way and they believe that the Lord is supposed to hear them and respond to them right away.

There are people who believe that the Lord doesn't know what they are going through in their lives from day to day, but the Lord knows what they will go through before they know.

There are people who believe that the Lord doesn't see them suffering from day to day, so they complain to the Lord as if the Lord is not on time to relieve them of their hardships.

There are people who believe that the Lord didn't hear their prayer the first time they prayed and asked the Lord to help them do what is right to do.

There are church folks who believe that the Lord is small, but the Lord is great and if it's in the Lord's will they will do great things in His holy name that is great in heaven.

There are people who believe that the Lord is not all-powerful and can't give them any power to speak words to cast demons out of captive souls who the devil can possess right in the church.

There are people who believe that the Lord is weak and won't provide for all of their needs, so day in and day out they complain to the Lord like He has failed them while the Lord is working it out for them to prosper even though they don't see it coming their way on the Lord's time not their time.

There are people who believe that they can look down on the Lord and put the Lord beneath them, telling the Lord to do whatever they want the Lord to do at their command.

The Lord is holy and righteous and all-powerful and perfect in all of His ways.

The demons know this and will tremble before the Lord, even when the weakest Christian calls on the name of the Lord Jesus Christ because the weakest Christian believes in the Lord who can remove the devil's stronghold from someone's life.

There are People, Even in the Church

There are people, even in the church, who have some devilish, slick and sly ways and you and I need to sincerely pray for these church folks who are supposed to be our brothers and sisters in the Lord.

There are people, even in the church, who can be jealous of you and me and can say indirect words to us that can cause you and me to feel like nothing, maybe because they feel like nothing.

You and I need the Holy Spirit to help us to discern those evil spirits that can possess many people right in the church where we are all broken people who only Jesus Christ can fix if we truly repent and turn to Him.

Back in the bible days, the religious people called the Pharisees tried to cause Jesus to look like He was nothing and feel like He was nothing because they could not cast out demons, heal the sick, feed the hungry, open the eyes of the blind and raise the dead.

Only Jesus had the power to do all of those things.

Those Pharisees were envious of Jesus and tried to cause Him to feel like nothing good at all by calling Jesus the devil and saying he was a blasphemer for saying that he could forgive people of their sins and because he said He was the Son of God.

It's nothing new today that there are people, even in the church, who can get jealous of you and me like Cain got jealous of his brother Abel and killed him because God didn't accept Cain's offerings.

The more you and I are like Jesus, the more there will be people, even in the church, who will try to cause us to look like nothing and feel like nothing because they are not giving Jesus all of their minds and hearts.

Jesus will show you and me who our true brothers and sisters in the church are, because Jesus Christ is the head of the church and separates the wheat from the tares.

All around the world the church is the best place to go to and hear the word of God for all believers in Jesus Christ.

At the same time, there will be people in those churches who are pretenders that are only going through the motions of praising the Lord when they actually have no renewed mind and heart in the Lord.

There are people, even in the church, who the devil is using to try to discourage you and me so that we feel like nothing in order to make themselves look so good, but this will not fool the Lord and His true children in the church.

It's So Easy

It's so easy for me to think wrong about you.

It's so easy for you to think wrong about me.

It's so easy for me to say something wrong about you.

It's so easy for you to say something wrong about me.

It's so easy for me to do you wrong.

It's so easy for you to do me wrong.

It's so easy for me to take you in the wrong way.

It's so easy for you to take me in the wrong way.

It's so easy for me to assume things about you.

It's so easy for you to assume things about me.

It's so easy for me to offend you.

It's so easy for you to offend me.

It's so easy for me to lie on you.

It's so easy for you to lie on me.

It's so easy for me to look at you in the wrong way.

It's so easy for you to look at me in the wrong way.

It's so easy for me to give you a bad look.

It's so easy for you to give me a bad look.

It's so easy for me to desire what you have.

It's so easy for you to desire what I have.

It's so easy for me to not be happy for you.

It's so easy for you to not be happy for me.

It's so easy for me to not care about what you say.

It's so easy for you to not care about what I say.

It's so easy for me to not care about what you do.

It's so easy for you to not care about what I do.

It's so easy for me to not care about how you feel.

It's so easy for you to not care about how I feel.

It's so easy for me to not want to get to know you.

It's so easy for you to not want to get to know me.

It's so easy for me to believe that I am better than you.

It's so easy for you to believe that you are better than me.

It's so easy for me to pretend that I don't see you.

It's so easy for you to pretend that you don't see me.

It's so easy for me to throw indirect words at you.

It's so easy for you to throw indirect words at me.

It's so easy for me to not like you.

It's so easy for you to not like me.

It's so easy for me to point my finger at your sins.

It's so easy for you to point your finger at my sins.

It's so easy for me to not want to be around you.

It's so easy for you to not want to be around me.

It's so easy for me to be on guard around you.

It's so easy for you to be on guard around me.

It's so easy for me to not know you, even in the church.

It's so easy for you to not know me, even in the church.

Even in the church, the heart can cover up wickedness and appear as an angel of light, but not to Jesus Christ, who is the head of the church to separate the wheat from the tares.

It's so easy for me to want to keep my distance from you.

It's so easy for you to want to keep your distance from me.

It's so easy for me to not forgive you.

It's so easy for you to not forgive me.

It's so easy for me to believe that you are good when you may be bad.

It's so easy for you to believe that I am good when I may be bad.

It's so easy for me to believe that you are bad, when you may be good.

It's so easy for you to believe that I am bad, when I may be good.

It's so easy for me to believe that you like me when you may dislike me.

It's so easy for you to believe that I like you when I may dislike you.

It's so easy for me to believe that I am a blessing to you when you may think of me as being a curse to you.

It's so easy for you to believe you are a blessing to me when I may think of you as being a curse to me.

Only the Lord can easily know our hearts, but you and I just don't always know even our own hearts.

The devil knows very easily where and how and when to tempt us to sin against God.

We are so blessed that Jesus came to this world to save us from our sins and not to condemn us in our sins that we can condemn ourselves in and be too hard on ourselves when we make a mistake that we can repent of and move on in making things right with Jesus.

We were all born in sin that makes it so easy for us to sin against God.

If anyone believes that it's hard to sin against God, then they are truly fooling themselves because God says that if a man says he has no sins, then he is a liar and the truth is not in him and that is so easy for truthful people to believe.

Doing Something Good for the Wrong Reason

Doing something good for the wrong reason will make anyone's actions deceptive.

Good actions will always look so right in many people's eyes from day to day that won't pass us by without knowing if anyone's actions are being true or pretense — only the Lord will always know.

Many people will do something good for the wrong reasons with their actions looking so pleasing to anyone who makes a practice of doing good things for the right reasons.

Many people will say that they can know people by their actions, but someone can have a bad action on the spur of the moment with a good reason — like killing someone in self-defense.

There is no good action in killing anyone, even if they are just downright evil, because the Lord says, "Thou shalt not kill."

When Cain killed his brother Abel, God put a mark on Cain making it so he could not be killed by anyone.

Doing something good for the wrong reason is nothing new today because back in the bible days Judas was portrayed as having good actions before Jesus' other disciples but Judas had the wrong reasons for being with Jesus.

Jesus truly knew that Judas' actions were deceptive and that Judas would betray Him, even though the other disciples didn't know because Judas' actions looked so right to them.

Many people believe that every action is true.

A serial killer portrays a good action by picking up a woman standing on the side of the road, but he has the wrong reason for doing this because he wants to kill her.

The woman doesn't know that his good action is deceptive until she gets into his car and he drives her to a remote area where she's never been and then kills her.

A good action can be full of pretense and you and I who call ourselves Christians need to pray without ceasing and study God's holy word and live by it with the help of the Holy Spirit so that we can always have good actions with the right reasons and be like Jesus in a sinful world full of many deceptive people who can portray good actions with the wrong reasons.

Only the Lord always sees these deceptions and will bring them to the light of His judgment.

What was the First Sin on Earth?

Was appetite or doubt the first sin on earth in the Garden of Eden where God told Adam and Eve not to eat from the tree of knowledge of good an evil?

Did the serpent cause doubt to enter into the mind of Eve and make her not believe that God had told her not to eat that unforbidden fruit?

Many people will say that appetite was the first sin against God here on earth, but what sin was in Adam and Eve's minds was to doubt the truth that God told them about staying away from that tree of knowledge of good and evil that was in the midst of the Garden of Eden.

Adam and Eve had to doubt what God told them before they ate the unforbidden fruit.

The serpent planted that seed of doubt in Eve's mind first, before Eve gave that unforbidden fruit to Adam to eat with her.

Once they ate, their eyes were opened to their sin of doubting the truth that God had told them about not eating the fruit.

The sin of doubt had entered into Adam and Eve's minds before they sinned against God with their mouths.

Do we do the same thing today when we doubt what the Lord tells us to say and do and don't do what the Lord has told us to do?

Did Lucifer doubt God up in heaven before he became proud of himself?

Did Lucifer doubt God and with thoughts of God not being worthy of worship from him, then convince one third of the angels in heaven to doubt God too before they were cast out of heaven?

Was doubt Lucifer's first sin against God and did it make him feel that God was unfair to the angels in heaven and to the other worlds?

Lucifer truly doubted God's supremacy over him, even though God was so good to him.

Lucifer took the fact that God was good to him as a sign of God's weakness and then tried to exalt himself above God.

If we doubt what the Lord can do for us, it will show and tell on you and me in a bad way and we will regret it.

Who has ever doubted the Lord and gotten away with it?

The sin of doubt always shows itself in some kind of way.

Adam and Eve's sin of doubting God was surely shown by their action of eating that unforbidden fruit.

Doubting God will breed pride, envy, selfishness, greed, foolishness, immorality, disobedience and lawlessness.

Lucifer was filled with all of these things and spread his doubt about God's love.

The proud will doubt God and put their trust in themselves, thinking they are perfect in their own eyes without thinking about God crushing their destiny in hell just like Lucifer didn't see the consequences for his actions coming his way until it was too late.

Even before Lucifer became filled with pride, he had begun to have doubts about God who created him perfect in all of his ways.

God had no doubts about creating Lucifer with a free will to love Him or rebel against Him.

Lucifer's doubts about God caused him to stray away from God up in heaven, then he spread his doubt to the other angels and caused one third of them to doubt God and rebel against him too.

Doubting God has a very strong hold on many people in this world today.

Even many church folks will doubt what the Lord God Jesus Christ can do for them if it's in God's will.

God's will is forever right for us and we should not doubt God who always knows what is best for us, even if we must die for His holy name's sake.

The demons won't doubt that they're powerless when we call on the name of Jesus.

Lucifer had doubts about God's love and thought it wasn't good enough for him, but we can thank Jesus for God's love being good enough for all the world to be saved in Jesus Christ.

Behind the Curtains of Life

We just don't know when we will die because we cannot see behind the curtains of life to know how and when we will die.

We don't see and don't know all of our enemies and we don't know who is talking bad about us because we cannot see behind the curtains of life.

We just don't know who is planning to do evil to us because we don't see the evil that may be very near to us behind the curtains of life.

We just don't know when an accident will come our way because we don't see the accident with our names written on it behind the curtains of life.

We just don't know what a day will bring because we cannot see even an extra second behind the curtains of life where we might breathe our last breath.

We just don't know what direction the Holy Spirit will direct our minds in because we don't see behind the curtains of life to know what the Holy Spirit will reveal to us.

We just don't know how the Lord will bless us because we cannot see behind the curtains of life to know how the Lord will bless us with something we've never seen before.

We just don't know who the Lord will send to us to help us because we cannot see behind the curtains of life; it could even be someone who comes to our church as a blessing from the Lord to us

We just don't know how far the Lord will take us in our lives because we cannot see behind the curtains of life, and we don't know how many souls we have pointed to Jesus who is far away from us up in heaven but is with us in His Holy Spirit and in His holy word.

We just don't know when Jesus will come back again because we cannot see behind the curtains of life, so we should always be ready and prepared to die for Jesus' holy name sake.

We just don't know our true heart's condition because we cannot see behind the curtains of life to see our unseen sins that we are ignorant of, but God will wink his eye at us to be washed clean in the blood of Jesus whose righteousness makes us right before God.

It's Always Good

No matter what we believe, it's always good to believe in Jesus Christ.

No matter what we go through in our lives, it's always good to deny ourselves and pick up our crosses to follow Jesus Christ.

No matter how we feel, it's always good to keep our trust in Jesus.

No matter how we are, it's always good to love Jesus and keep His Commandments.

No matter how much we achieve in life, it's always good to give Jesus all the glory and praise.

No matter how many enemies we have, it's always good to live for Jesus.

No matter what hardships we've been through in our lives, it's always good to give testimonies about Jesus bringing us through our bad days.

No matter what is going on in this world, it's always good to keep our eyes fixed on Jesus.

No matter how much the devil tries to tempt us, it's always good to call on the name of Jesus.

No matter how long we live, it's always good to do the Lord's will.

No matter how close we get to Jesus, it's always good to confess our sins.

No matter how good we are, it's always good to acknowledge that Jesus is good all the time above our good that our neighbors can despise.

No matter how healthy we are, it's always good for our body to be the holy temple of God.

No matter how good our lives are, it's always good to pray to Jesus.

No matter how well we know the bible scriptures, it's always good to have a relationship with Jesus.

No matter how much we work for Jesus, it's always good to be saved in Jesus because our works can't save us.

The Church is for Sinners Like Me and You

The church is for sinners like me and you to repent and turn to Jesus Christ who is the head of the church which is His bride and he will take her to heaven when He comes back again on the clouds of glory.

The church is for sinners like me and you to assemble ourselves together to worship the Lord who gives us His Holy spirit to renew our lives for us to be Christians one day at a time.

The church is for sinners like me and you to confess our sins unto the Lord who will cleanse us of our sins so we can be more and more like Him.

When we become a Christian, it doesn't mean that we are perfect to have no more sins to confess and repent of unto the Lord.

The church is for sinners like me and you to love Jesus and keep His Commandments and to love one another to be Jesus' disciples before unbelievers every day.

The church is for sinners like me and you to be like Jesus Christ, which only a Christian can be like inside and outside the church day after day.

You and I are supposed to be a living example of Jesus for unbelievers so they can see Jesus in me and you.

The church is for sinners like me and you who can only be saved in Jesus one day at a time — just because we are saved it doesn't mean that we are always saved in Jesus Christ.

The church is for sinners like me and you who are so spiritually sick without Jesus and are so messed up in our selfish ways that only Jesus can cleanse us from because we have a relationship with Him.

The church is for sinners like me and you who were born in sin and can easily sin against the Lord, even right in the church that is truly the right place for us to enter into and hear about the Lord who can transform anyone's life for believing in Him.

The church is for sinners like me and you who were not born a Christian but were born a sinner who needs to have a spiritual surgery on our hearts so Jesus can cut out our sins and renew our lives to be like Him.

The church is for sinners like me and you to give Jesus all the glory and praise because only Jesus Christ, our Lord, is worthy to be the King of our lives beyond our sinful nature that needs a lifetime of sanctification in the church of Jesus Christ.

Only Jesus Christ was born without sin to have no sins for Him to be the head of the church over you and me who would cause the church to go to hell if we were the head of the church.

Spiritually Oppressed

There are many people who are emotionally oppressed by getting their hearts broken over and over again because of being in an out of relationships with the wrong kind of people

There are many people who are psychologically oppressed by thinking so negative day after day, especially about the bad things that they are going through in their lives.

There are many people who are financially oppressed by being in debt and not being able to pay their bills, especially if they're out of a job.

There are many people who are physically oppressed by a sickness in their bodies for years and years.

There are many people who are mentally oppressed by a sickness in their minds causing them to miss out on reality in the real world where being in one's right mind is the ultimate survival from day to day.

You and I can be spiritually oppressed right in the church if we don't keep our eyes fixed on Jesus Christ.

There are people in the church who will speak words of freedom in Jesus, but they can still spiritually oppress you and me with their lack of encouragement for you and me.

You and I shouldn't spiritually oppress one another in the household of faith where our actions can spiritually oppress especially those who are weak in their faith in Jesus Christ.

You and I can talk about Jesus all we want to, but if our actions are not like Jesus then we are spiritually oppressing one another because we must have love for one another to be Jesus' disciples for the world to see that we are truly free from living in sin because of being saved in Jesus Christ.

You and I can be right in the church and be spiritually oppressed, which is the worst kind of oppression and can cause our souls to be lost.

If we don't love one another all the same, then we are spiritually oppressed in our showing respect of persons to not be like Jesus who loves everybody all the same because He gave up His life on the cross to save everybody from their sins to redeem us back to God. There is no big you and little me in God's holy eyesight that looks down on us from heaven and sees us all needing to be set free from the spiritual oppression of sin being filled with nothing but evil words and actions day by day.

You and I who call ourselves Christians are so blessed that Jesus Christ is the head of the church to set us free from spiritual oppression for us to be like Him that we can't do on our own without His Holy Spirit living in us.

From up in the pulpit and down through all the pews in the church, spiritual oppression can press us all down in some kind of seen and unseen way, but we can truly thank God for Jesus who is all about setting us all free from spiritually oppressing ourselves in the illusion of proudness being nothing new because of Lucifer's choosing to spiritually oppress himself by wanting to exalt himself above God in heaven.

Because of You, my Lord

Because of You, my Lord, my good days outnumber my bad days.

Because of You, my Lord, my good days are more brilliant than my bad days.

Because of You, my Lord, my good days are smarter than my bad days.

Because of You, my Lord, my good days are bigger than my bad days.

Because of You, my Lord, my good days are taller than my bad days.

Because of You, my Lord, my good days are higher than my bad days.

Because of You, my Lord, my good days are wider than my bad days.

Because of You, my Lord, my good days are longer than my bad days.

Because of You, my Lord, my good days are stronger than my bad days.

Because of You, my Lord, my good days are sharper than my bad days.

Because of You, my Lord, my good days are faster than my bad days.

Because of You, my Lord, my good days are more real than my bad days.

Because of You, my Lord and Savior Jesus Christ, my good days are more talented than my bad days that fall down into their own deep pit, but Jesus answering my prayers is always on time for my bad days to tremble in fear.

Nothing Can

Nothing can help us better than the truth.

Nothing can help us like the truth.

Nothing can set us more free than the truth.

Nothing can strengthen us like the truth.

Nothing can be more encouraging than the truth.

Nothing can heal us like the truth.

Nothing can energize us like the truth.

Nothing can help us to see things clearly like the truth.

Nothing can ease our minds more than the truth.

Nothing makes us guilty like the truth.

Nothing builds us up like the truth.

Nothing cheers us like the truth.

Nothing makes us feel good like the truth.

Nothing keeps us going like the truth.

Nothing helps us to see deceptions like the truth.

Nothing makes our lives much better like the truth.

Nothing can be more loving than the truth.

Nothing can help us to know who we are like the truth.

Nothing can show us our sins like the truth.

Nothing can help us to move on in life like the truth.

Nothing can help us to get through the day like the truth.

Nothing can help us to get the victory like the truth.

Nothing turns our lives around like the truth.

Nothing can be more good to us than the truth.

Nothing can help us to know God like the truth in His holy word.

Nothing can help us to be like Jesus more than the truth that is Jesus Christ whose love for us is so true every day that the Holy Spirit teaches all truth about Jesus Christ.

Nothing can make us spiritually well like the truth of God's holy word that the devil loves to make to be a lie when God cannot lie to you and me who will lie to the truth if we don't love Jesus and keep His Commandments.

Nothing can love us more than the truth because the truth is that God so loved the world that He gave us His only begotten Son that whosoever believeth in Him shall not perish but shall have everlasting life.

Nothing can love us like the truth because God is love and so loved us first to be the truth of God's holy word being like a love letter from God to us to know the truth about the one and only self-existing God in His Son, Jesus Christ, and in the Holy Spirit who are three persons in one God to be a deep mystery of eternal truth.